The Smartt View:

Life, Love, and Cluttered Closets

By Lisa Smartt

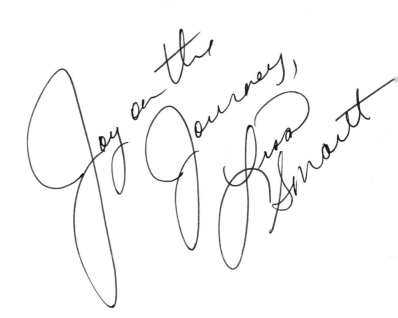

Joy on the Journey,
Lisa Smartt

A Compilation of Weekly Newspaper Columns Originally Published in "The Weakley County Press" and "The Union City Daily Messenger"

www.lisasmartt.com

Front cover photograph by Stacey Baker, Baby Pix Photography

To Philip,
Your remarkable life has inspired every word of this
book.

To Stephen and Jonathan,
Thanks for bringing such chaos and laughter to our
family! Watching you grow into men will be our
all-too-soon privilege.

Acknowledgements

Special thanks to my mom and dad, Jack and Regina Golden. Mom, a brilliant writer, has been my advisor, counselor, proof reader, mentor, and friend. Dad gave me the gift of laughter and taught me the joys of never meeting a stranger. They both have supported this project with their encouragement and their prayers. Thanks to my parents, I've never spent one moment of my life wondering if I were loved.

Sylvia Smartt, my mother-in-law, makes all the mother-in-law jokes in the world seem ridiculous. She was my friend and supporter long before I met her son. I'll never forget the prayers she prayed asking God to give me a wonderful husband. She had no idea she was praying for her son and that someday she and I would have the privilege of being "family." Her prayers and love have sustained me for more than twenty years.

Kim Lightfoot has been my soul sister in parenting, dieting, flawed housecleaning and poor pet maintenance. But mostly, she has been an invaluable sister in Christ through the laughter and the tears of this life.

I would also like to acknowledge Carolyn Thomason, my sixth grade teacher, who fueled my enthusiasm for writing.

Special thanks to the Sunday night Bible Study group. Their prayers, love, laughter, and encouragement have kept our family going.

The Union City Daily Messenger and The Weakley County Press have faithfully printed my weekly column for more than three years. They gave me a reason to push through my procrastinating nature and keep writing.

Above all, I give praise to God. His creation amazes. His creativity inspires. His incredible love has brought such joy and laughter to the world.

Table of Contents

Chapter 1

Did I Say That?: Confessions of a Human Being

Dental Confessions

I've confessed my tendency to overeat. I've expressed my imperfections as a mom. But, nothing is more embarrassing than the confessions I'm prepared to make today. Dental confessions.

If my dentist is reading this and you know who you are, I'm prepared to come clean. I don't floss. And by the way, LOTS of people don't floss. If they say they floss daily, I think a security camera should be installed in their home to provide proof.

And here's another painful confession. I usually only brush my teeth in the morning. Oh sure. I put on a good front. When I'm at a women's retreat, I rush to the bathroom at 9:00 p.m. with all the other ladies as though I'm desperate for my nightly teeth brushing ritual. It's all just a scam. A horrible scam. At home, I usually just hop in the bed at night. If romance is in the air? Scope. Yeah. Even the throws of romance don't motivate prying that toothbrush out of the drawer at night. A little swish and spit of Scope. Good to go. And it's not even a fluoride rinse. The shame of it all.

I don't know who to blame for my dental hygiene inadequacies. Perhaps I need to see a therapist about it. My parents are wonderful and highly disciplined people. We went for those yearly check-ups. They made us brush. Now it's come to this.

And it's not that I haven't had to pay for my dental crimes. Oh no. We've paid. Fillings. Root canals. Crowns and the like. I've filled the coffers of many a fine dentist (and some not so fine) throughout several different states. And still I haven't learned. But, this brings a question to mind. What if I

HAD done what all dentists had told me to do? What if ALL of us had forever done what all dentists had told us to do? What if we ate no sweets, brushed three times a day, flossed religiously? What if we even used one of those water toothbrushes that uses a Niagara Falls-like flood of cleaning power to eliminate plaque and tartar? Yeah. What if we had? Dentists encourage us to do all those things knowing all the while that their business is dependent on us NOT doing those things. A precarious situation at best.

Don't worry. I'm not opposed to good dentistry. Are you kidding? I'm the poster child for good dentistry. I'd be missing teeth and in constant pain were it not for the meticulous skills of good dentists. Dentists are wonderful professionals in my book. They're amazing. They're unbelievable. I think a dentist should become president. (And if this public exhortation causes my dentist to want to give me a 10% discount, so be it.)

I'm writing this column to let all of you know I'm turning over a new leaf. This ol' dog is learning a new trick. I'm going to start flossing daily and brushing my teeth at night. I'm serious. I'm tired of paying out the nose for my bad habits. Come join me, West Tennesseans. We'll start a dental hygiene movement. We can pass out free floss and dental hygiene pamphlets in parking lots.

At the age of 40, I've learned my lesson. And by the way, those of you following my struggle with weight, I've lost 13 lbs. Yep! I'm eating low carb and I'm going to be a daily flosser. What's next? Anybody know how to reconcile a checkbook?

Automation Aggravation

I need to learn patience. I need to let things go. I need to be a kinder, gentler Lisa. I'd like to take this time to thank my health insurance company for revealing my impatience and for showing me the light. Breathe in. Breathe out. I've discovered something about myself. I like real people. As aggravating as human beings can sometimes be, I still prefer them to voice automation systems. I've battled with the automated insurance monster and lived to tell the tale.

A doctor in Jackson had recommended that our younger son undergo a 12-week round of vision therapy. I still don't know what vision therapy is exactly. So, I called our insurance company to ask what seemed like such a simple question, "Do you cover vision therapy?" I had no idea the automated insurance monster was waiting to consume me.

The automated female voice was deceptively pleasant, "Hello and welcome to _____Insurance Company. We look forward to assisting you. Are you a pharmacist, a member or a provider?"

This was going to be so easy. I cheerfully said into the phone, "A member."

"Did you say member?"

"Yes, I said member."

"I'm sorry. I didn't understand you. Did you say member?"

"YES! I said member!"

"Would you like to learn more about a current bill or would you like to learn about eligibility benefits?"

"Eligibility benefits."

"I'm sorry. I didn't understand you. Please try again."

"ELIGIBILITY BENEFITS!!"

And in the same deceptively pleasant voice, "Did you say eligibility benefits? If you said eligibility benefits, please press one now." I gladly pressed one. I had made it to Round Two with the automated insurance monster and I wasn't even sweating.

The same female voice said, "I'm going to read you a list of benefits and services. When you hear the benefit or service you're interested in, please just say that benefit. Thank you. Would you like to know more about in-office procedures, pharmacy coverage, vision coverage…"

This was my chance. With my most articulate voice I calmly said, "Vision."

"Did you say bone fusion? If you said bone fusion, press one now."

"No, I said vision!"

"Did you say bone fusion? If you said bone fusion, press one now."

"No, I said VISION! VISION! VISION!"

"Did you say renal failure? If you said renal failure, please press one now."

"NO! Not bone fusion, not renal failure. VISION! And check benefits for high blood pressure while you're at it!!"

"I'm sorry. I can't understand what you're saying. Please say it again."

That was it. The automated monster had given me a right hook to the jaw and I was lying on the mat helpless. Down for the count. Bloodied and bruised by her calm and deceptively pleasant automated voice, it looked like she was the victor. But, no. I couldn't give up.

I had one last hope and I had it to use it. I pulled myself up by the ropes and stood tall. I donned the boxing gloves and held the phone out a few feet from my mouth. "HUMAN BEING!! HUMAN BEING! SO HELP ME, FIND A HUMAN AND PUT THAT HUMAN ON THIS PHONE!! HUMAN BEING! HUMAN BEING!"

And finally, she heard me. She understood me. I was one with the automated monster. "I believe you may need an associate. Would you like to speak to one of our associates? If you'd like to speak to one of our associates, please press one."

I was in. Perseverance. Tenacity. "Hi. My name is Don. How can I help you?"

"Just one question, Don. Does my insurance cover anger management?"

I'm Not Running for Public Office

I've seen the political ads on TV. And I've made a decision. I'm not running for public office. Too many skeletons in the closet.

A woman with double-chin Christmas morning pictures and questionable relatives could never survive the current climate of ad campaigns. I can just see my opponent's TV spot. A blown-up picture of me in my penguin pajamas while dramatic quotes are flashed onto the screen. "Lisa Smartt SAYS she'll work for you. But Lisa's 3rd grade teacher has a different story."

My 3rd grade teacher, now elderly and wearing curlers and a muumuu appears on screen, "Lisa was a loud girl. She could never find her inside voice. And by the way, I've checked my records and she never turned in pg. 47 in the math workbook."

ANNOUNCER (In a dramatic voice): "If Lisa Smartt can't turn in her math page...what makes you think she can balance a budget?"

Then there would be the interview with the police officer in Clarksburg: "Yes, Lisa Smartt is a law breaker. Even as I speak, she's awaiting her day in court. While she nervously fumbled through maps and bank receipts looking for her registration, I noticed her wheel wells were littered with Sonic cups and school fundraiser catalogs."

Announcer: "Lisa Smartt rarely turns in school fundraising packets on time. Lisa Smartt has a weakness for limeades. Lisa Smartt. Today it's just a messy 4-door Saturn speeding through a small Tennessee town. Tomorrow it could be a messy scandal jeopardizing your children's future."

They'd find my college roommate to get her on-camera recollections, "I'm not saying Lisa Smartt is an evil person.

I'm saying she's a bit disheveled and unorganized. I hesitate to mention this, but she often wore the same pair of socks two days in a row because she didn't want to do her laundry."

Announcer: "Lisa Smartt SAYS she'll clean up government waste….but she can't even clean her OWN socks. What other dirty laundry is in her closet?"

But by far the scariest part of running for public office is the fact that opponents might try to get too up close and personal with my family members. Interviews with second cousins at RV parks around the country. Undercover reporters watching my parents tote in their own box of Raisin Bran at motels. The mental pictures are frightening. One picture keeps popping into my mind. My boys wearing red cowboy boots, shorts, and orange tank tops standing next to my husband wearing dark socks and his 1983 aqua swimsuit and camouflage shirt.

Announcer: "Lisa Smartt wants to represent you. Lisa Smartt says she'll go the distance for you. But would you want a woman who dresses her family like THIS to represent YOU and YOUR family? Lisa Smartt. She's loud. She's a limeade-drinkin', penguin pajama-clad, dirty-sock wearer. And her husband? He's a camouflage-wearing college professor. Camouflage? What's he trying to hide? Lisa Smartt. Isn't it time we asked for more?"

It's easy to make fun of political commercials. Some are tasteless while others border on the ridiculous. But the mud-slinging ads don't make me half as sad as the possibility that naïve people may be trusting a clever 60-second commercial for political information. Elections are much more serious than choosing breakfast cereal. Get the facts. Do your research. Exercise your right to vote. I'm Lisa Smartt. And in a caffeine-induced state, while wearing penguin pajamas, I approve this message.

My Blue Light Special

I'm a law breaker. I'm guilty. I did it. I teach my boys about following laws, respecting rules, and obeying authority. Now they've experienced a lesson in what happens when those laws are violated. Unfortunately, I taught them that lesson myself. Both boys were happily strapped in the backseat wearing matching Spiderman suits when the blue lights came on. The painful and innocent question soon surfaced, "Mom, why is the policeman following us with his lights on?" Ouch. Yeah. Why is that?

My response was as cool as a cucumber, "Honey, I think I was speeding back there OR maybe he just wants me to pull over so he can speed past me and chase down a dangerous and fugitive bank robber." But alas, no fugitives in sight.

The officer was nice and respectful. They're almost always nice and respectful. No offense, but the kindness makes it worse. You almost wish the policeman would say, "Gee, this is going to be a BAD day for you, Mrs. Smartt. First of all, you're embarrassed in front of your kids. Now, I'm going to get in my car and write you a really expensive speeding ticket. THEN, to top it all off, you're going to have to go home and admit to your husband that you were driving 22 miles per hour OVER the speed limit RIGHT in front of the Weakley Co. Sheriff's Dept. Oh yeah, Mrs. Smartt, you're going to regret this one in a BIG way." But of course, the officer didn't say that. He introduced himself as though we were at Rotary Club. I expected some free bar-b-q and peach cobbler. None came.

I'm sure the nice officer was relieved that he didn't know me. I always feel sorry for small town police officers in that regard. To me, it would be a painful thing to pull someone over and then get out of the police car and say, "Hey George, how's the wife and kids? I saw that oldest one of yours playing Little League the other night. Yeah. He's got quite an arm there. Okay. Well, I've gotta run back here and write you a really expensive speeding ticket. I'll be back in a minute." That seems like a slightly uncomfortable situation to me. I take it there was no pain involved in writing my ticket.

Like all people caught in a violation, I feel the need to blame someone. I choose Ned Ray McWherter. That's the best I can do. The information I've been given is that the former governor is responsible for some of the great highways we have in W. Tennessee. Let's be honest. Hwy. 22 is wide and smooth.....like the Autobahn. The Germans would be embarrassed to ask people to drive 45 mph on the Autobahn. It would be like clipping an eagle's wings.

I know it's irrational to blame Mr. McWherter. He wasn't driving a red Saturn like a maniac past the Sheriff's Dept. in Dresden with two spidermen in the backseat. No. That was me, I'm afraid.

There's a phone number on the back of the ticket in case I want to find out the amount of the fine and just mail it in. But I think that would be a great injustice to the readers of this column. Every writer should be willing to experience the discomforts of life so as to report about them. In a few weeks, I'll be writing about my experience in traffic court. We'll see how my Ned Ray McWherter defense plays out. I feel hopeful.

A Day in Traffic Court

Some of you read my column a few months ago detailing my brush with the law. For those of you who missed it, let me give you a quick overview. In late October, I was speeding down Highway 22 when the blue lights came on. My sons, dressed in Spiderman suits and sitting calmly in the backseat, quickly learned the consequences of violating the laws of our great country. My crime meant I would eventually spend an afternoon in traffic court. I promised readers a detailed description of traffic court. Today I'm prepared to deliver.

For those of you who have never been caught in a traffic violation, let this column be a stern warning to you to stay vigilantly on the path of good. Don't be tempted to take a walk on the wild side. Oh no. Be assured you will end up as I did...sitting in general sessions court, awaiting your verdict.

It was a wintry December day when I arrived at the designated location in downtown Dresden. When I walked in the room, it was already filled with violators like me. Though the room was full, it was deathly quiet. Most people stared at the carpet or the ceiling. I don't like quiet in situations like this. I'm not sure why. This is a trait I got from my dad. He talks to people in elevators, gas stations, and airports. I believe when human beings are together there should be conversation and camaraderie. The judge had not yet arrived, so I engaged in conversation with others who were also awaiting judgment. I enjoyed the people I met and learned a lot about this county. Had we been given a little more time, I believe we would have held hands and sung Kum-ba-yah. Maybe not.

The judge was late for court. I'm prepared to give him the benefit of the doubt, believing he was engaged in crucial legal matters which made us regular traffic violators seem like small

19

potatoes. At one point, while we were waiting, I polled the room to see if it would be wise or unwise to mention his tardiness. The consensus was clear. We would keep the judge's tardiness to ourselves and put on happy faces upon his arrival.

The judge arrived and I liked him immediately because he had a sense of humor. I liked the way he dealt with people. He seemed balanced in his approach. He wanted violators to feel bad about what they had done, but not totally humiliated. One young man stands out in my mind. He had passed a school bus while it was unloading. The judge took the time to make SURE he understood the seriousness of the violation. As a citizen and a mom, I appreciate that.

I'll now share another fact which should deter all readers from a life of traffic crime. All the violators actually sit and listen while the judge talks to you and hands down your penalty. I'm serious. He just calls your name and then you have to sit in a chair and discuss your violation while the rest of the crowd looks on. Be prepared.

When my name was called, I sat in the chair and pronounced myself guilty as sin. I had no intention of trying to defend my actions. I did, however, thoroughly enjoy the conversation with the judge. He asked if I made speeding a habit. I told him I had stayed pretty clean from ages 30-41. However, I confessed that my teens and early 20's were awash with speeding violations. I also confessed that many women hit a sort of "second adolescence" in their 40's though I had no intention of entering into a life of speeding crime myself.

I asked if there were any mercy for people who were new in the area and I loved his quick response. He said, "Sure, if you come from an area where there are no speed limits."

I replied, "I certainly don't come from an area where they would build a road that looked like the Autobahn...and then put up a 45 m.p.h. speed limit sign." He laughed and then handed down his judgment. And, of course, I won't be able to tell you what that judgment was. Let me just leave you with the last and most important fact about traffic court. Always bring the checkbook.

Chapter 2

Parenting: The Good, the Bad, and the Ugly

Back to School Blues

My boys aren't finished with summer. They don't understand why school has to barge into their lives interfering with squirrel chasing, rock throwing, and other essential activities. First grade and fourth grade don't promise experiences nearly as exciting as chasing each other with sticks while yelling, "You're going down! Intruders must be eliminated!" Running with sticks is just plain frowned upon in the hallways of most public schools.

I know. Lots of you have kids who just love school. I hear about it all the time. You're the ones I see in the school supply aisle. You and your child are just giddy with excitement as you pick out the perfect Scooby-Doo folder and matching lunch box. When I say something about how quickly summer has passed, you make comments like, "Oh, my little Jolene is just dying to get back into the classroom." OR "Junior is just SO excited about school and academic achievement that he asks every day if it's time to go back." That's when you look at me. You know that look. You're waiting for me to tell you how excited my kids are, too.

Instead, I say, "My boys would rather dig in a mud hole."

You smile and say, "Boys will be boys." But I know what you're thinking. It's all over your face. You're thinking, "Your boys will be working for my kid someday." Maybe so. I can assure you of one thing. If your kid promises one of my boys a job which comes with a mud hole, a grilled cheese sandwich every day, and no required handwriting, he'll consider it a gift!

There are several reasons that school doesn't fit into my boys' current lifestyle of choice. But the primary reason for both of them is clear. Handwriting. Whatever it is that families do to promote a love of handwriting, we forgot to do it. Too late now. They hate handwriting. If we want to discipline them in the most intense, cruel and agonizing way, we just threaten them with a pencil and a piece of paper. Behavior improves dramatically. They'd rather haul wood and pull weeds than sit and do handwriting. I know. Some of you have kids who love handwriting. Your child voluntarily kept a daily journal this summer. She wrote long letters to Grandma and even drew pictures. Maybe your children are even competing in national penmanship contests. Congratulations. However, I need to prepare you for something. If the National "Dig Yourself out of a Mud Hole" contest comes to town, my boys are primed and ready for victory.

Another thing school is famous for promoting is the value of sitting still and staying focused. Let me caution you parents out there. Mud hole digging, while a perfectly worthy activity, does not prepare young people for sitting still and staying focused. Just trust me on this one. First hand experience.

Maybe my boys don't want to go to school because they find my presence so terribly engaging. That's it, I'm sure. It's not the handwriting or the sitting still. They probably just can't stand the thought of not gleaning my constant verbal wisdom all during the day. Here's some of my coveted "summer words of wisdom": "This stinks. Put it in the hamper." "This stinks. Put it in the trash can." "You stink. Put yourself in the tub."

I'm not worried about my boys' current lack of academic enthusiasm. I've no doubt they'll look back on their elementary years with fondness. It's OK that they look at "back to school" season as a mild inconvenience. Thankfully, their destiny is not determined by elementary school achievements. They're both learners. Curious. Industrious. Wide-eyed. I choose to believe their destiny is not in jeopardy. Not even close. My boys, with all their strengths and weaknesses, will find a way to make it through first grade and fourth grade. As long as the teachers keep them away from sticks and mud holes, they'll be just fine.

Parents Who Fear Homework

"Mom, can you help me with my homework?"

"Sure, Honey! I'll be right there."

As I turn the dining room corner to impart my parental wisdom, I gasp in horror because I see it sitting out in the open on our dining room table. A large book which says MATH in big bold letters. Oh sure, there's a bright graphic of a friendly dinosaur on the cover which tries to make it look innocent enough. But it won't fool me. I know family-traumatizing contraband when I see it. My face turns pale and my palms become sweaty. I want to speak but my dry mouth will allow no words to escape. That's when I fear that my sweet little innocent prodigy will say something like, "Mom, if Dan walks 3.9 miles west and Susan walks 8.2 miles south and Carl walks 7.1 miles south southwest and they each have $1.89 in their pockets..." The room starts spinning and the colors are all a blur. Flashbacks. Tragic flashbacks to my own childhood. Crying. Math books flying through the air. The pale green Formica on our childhood kitchen table. Math-loving parents trying to help me see the light. Memories it would take years of therapy to erase. And now here we are. The forced re-living of it all.

That's when I innocently clear my throat and say, "I think Dad will be home soon and he just LOVES a good math problem. I'd hate to steal the joy from him. I'm just that kind of person. Let's do a special favor for Dad by saving the Math homework for him. How's that sound? I mean, don't you have any English homework, Sweetie? We might need to practice those spelling words."

"Mom, I don't have English homework. Dad won't be home for another hour. Why don't you want to help me?" As I feel my blood pressure rising, I hear the confession come spilling from my mouth like Niagara Falls, "You see, Honey. Well. There's something you should know about your mom. Uh. I knew we'd have to have this talk someday. Maybe I was hoping it would be later rather than sooner. But, anyway, you see, there are things about me that I've never told you. We all make mistakes in life, right? Sweetheart, it's time I come clean. There's really no other way to say it. Your mom is…well…Math challenged." There. I said it. I place my head in my hands and begin to weep uncontrollably. The secret is out. Somehow it feels good deep down in my soul to be free of the pretenses of parental mathematical ability. Freedom. Sweet freedom.

The silence is deafening. Waiting. Wondering if my child will lose that sense of child-like wonder and idealism he feels concerning his mother. And then he speaks, "Oh Mom, I know you're not good at math. I mean, I figured that out a long time ago. You cringe every time the 'Math Made Easy' infomercial comes on. Your face gets blotchy when you mention your College Algebra class. Mom, I've seen you turn pale when you try to reconcile your checkbook. You lose your car in the Wal-Mart parking lot. You can't even figure out which door to take out of a public restroom."

"That's fine, Honey. I think we all get the picture."

"Mom, we all know you have mathematical and spatial challenges. And don't worry. I wasn't expecting you to understand how to do this word problem."

"You weren't?"

"Oh, no way. Are you kidding? I knew this problem would blow your mind. I was just going to ask you how to spell 'direction.'"

Housecoat Parenting

Some things just shouldn't be done after 9 p.m. Parenting, for instance. No offense to my lovely boys but, I'm done with them by 9 p.m. I'm going on 14 hours of parenting at that point…and it's time to call it a day. Unless you have an infant or a child over 12 years old, no parenting should ever occur after 9 p.m. None. Trust me. I've tried to parent after 9 p.m. It's downright ugly. Many articles have been written about the benefits of regular, early bedtimes for children. The reasons sited are often: 1. Children need a lot of rest. 2. Most children benefit from structure and routine. 3. Regular bedtimes improve school performance.

That's all fine and good. But I think they left out one of the most important reasons of all for early bedtimes for children. Parental hysteria. I can't parent effectively late at night. It's what I call "housecoat parenting." "Housecoat parenting" is never good. Stop and think about it. Late at night your child comes to you and says, "I forgot to tell you I'm supposed to dress up like Yankee Doodle Dandy tomorrow for the school play and I signed up to bring 6 dozen homemade brownies." The wrath of a tired parent is slowly creeping through your body. Smoke is coming out of your ears and you can feel the "You MUST be more responsible" speech on the tip of your tongue. Let me guess. You're in your housecoat, right? Right.

OK. Here's another scenario. It's 6 a.m. when your child comes running into the kitchen. You haven't even had your coffee yet. The child begins to chatter away about how underprivileged he is because he doesn't have an X-box or some other over-priced mind-numbing object which will almost insure that he will never read the works of Ernest Hemingway. With bad breath and a caffeine-deprived attitude, you tell him there's no way he's getting an X-Box. You also remind him that when you were his age, you worked in the fields and were happy with a corn cob doll and 3 square meals a day. Yep! You were definitely in your housecoat.

I've tried to explain to my children that they need to approach me with emotional traumas or serious requests during the day when I have on regular clothes. If it's after 9 p.m. and I've had a warm bath and I'm in my housecoat curled up with a good book, the only comment I want to hear from my children is, "Yes, Mommy, we brushed our teeth. Our room is immaculate. Our homework is completed and you are the greatest mother on the face of the earth." Anything more strenuous than that just seems to push me over the edge of the parenting cliff. If it's before 7 a.m. and I'm drinking coffee while wearing my housecoat, I want to hear nothing more stressful than, "Good morning, Mommy! What a lovely day to excel academically. Thank God for such a great family!"

Dealing with serious parental issues while wearing a housecoat is just dangerous and wrong. It may be that the housecoat itself removes an air of "parental authority" from us. Maybe we feel a little insecure and therefore we over-compensate with ranting and raving. Come to think of it, that makes sense. I'm not sure how seriously I would take the counsel of someone wearing a terrycloth Sponge Bob robe and Bugs Bunny slippers. Maybe that's why we "turn up the volume" a little when we're wearing sleepwear.

If you're not already convinced that your kids should be in bed long before 9 p.m., let me share the final exhortation. Parents aren't the only ones at fault here. Kids aren't very likeable after 9 p.m. either. Think about it. They get bent out of shape a little easier than usual. My kids have cried over toothpaste. They've fought over who got to wear the dinosaur pajamas. And of course, their mom was wearing a housecoat so they got the "You should just be happy you've got pajamas, MISTER!" speech.

Parenting is a joyous privilege. But no one said it would be easy. If anyone thinks parenting is easy, feel free to write to me. I'll send you back a scathing reply explaining your delusion. And when you read it, you'll know. I was wearing my housecoat.

Teenagers and Brand-New Cars

My parents owe me a big apology. They conned me. They convinced me that teenagers were supposed to drive old cars in honor of long-held traditions which supported our American way of life. They made it clear that new cars were for adults who had real jobs. Teenagers drove the cars that people with real jobs no longer wanted. This was the system that made America great. People with real jobs could drive new or nearly new cars. Teenagers drove old cars which could be mangled and wrecked with little or no emotional trauma. This was the philosophy my parents taught. This was the philosophy I came to believe.

It was the fall of 1979 when I first started cruising the streets of Denton, Texas. I was the picture of cool in my first real set of wheels...a 1973 white Gremlin with a faded pink racing stripe. (Racing stripe is just a figure of speech.) 0-45 in 10 minutes flat. $250 worth of pure mechanical genius. The ignition didn't even require a key which was great for a person like me who can't keep up with keys anyway. Even though no key was required, the 1973 white Gremlin with the faded pink racing stripe was never stolen. I know. Sheerly amazing.

My philosophy about old cars was tested my junior year when my best friend was given a brand new car by her parents. Such a shame really. Like giving a kid an ice cream cone right before dinner...and wondering why he complains about the baked chicken. A teenager driving a Gremlin is a teenager who is hopeful about the future. A teenager driving a brand-new car is a teenager whose future has already come. It's all down hill from there.

I've heard a lot lately about teenagers who drive brand-new or nearly new cars. It seems to be a trend. This phenomenon makes me believe my parents need to do a seminar explaining why teenagers driving brand-new cars opposes the American way of life. They could do late-night infomercials. The seminar could be called, "Driving Grandma's Car...the Joys of Being 16 in America." This could be a helpful service to parents who are afraid to tell their kids "no." If parents in America would join hands and develop a unified mission statement, life could get back to normal. 16-year-olds would be driving big grandma cars or old trucks. Maybe Gremlins could even be re-introduced into society on behalf of teenagers who need the experience. I just want to share the joy.

There are lots of things in life that money can't buy. My husband and I recently saw a TV show about a family who spent $3500 on a 7-year-old's birthday party. I'm not sure what they were trying to buy. But I have a feeling they didn't get it. Dr. Phil McGraw says it best in his book, "Family First:" "I don't know for certain how it happened, but many parents have bought into their children's sense of entitlement. Some operate under the theory that they're better parents if they spare their children any difficult times or challenges. Today, many parents feel guilty when they cannot buy their children expensive designer clothes, new cars and the latest high-tech toys that young people demand. The kids don't know any better. But we should."

Someday my boys are going to ask for a car. They're going to explain why it's safer and more sensible for us to buy them a brand-new truck or car. They're going to bring home brochures and they're going to plan speeches. As for us, we already have a plan. We're going to listen carefully and sensitively. Then, with great unity, we're going to explain to them some of the philosophies that have made America great. We're going to stand strong. We're going to tell them how much we love them as we embark on a nationwide search for a Gremlin.

Learning to Ride a Bike

Coordination has never been one of my strong points. For me, learning to ride a bike was an almost unnatural pursuit. Kind of like Julie Andrews learning to sing rap music. It's not that it can't be done…but it might take a while. I'm sure everyone in my family was wondering if there would ever be a resolution to my childhood "bicycle dilemma." I can still picture every detail of the drama. Summer nights would find me perched on the hill behind our house attempting to ride my brother's green bike with the white banana seat. My family cheered me on…despite the inevitable blood-curdling wreckage that would follow each attempt. I have a feeling that despite their encouraging cheers, they were tempted to say, "Honey, you're good at lots of things. No really, you are. But it's become clear to all of us that some people simply weren't designed to ride a bike. Go figure. Sweetheart, you may be one of those 'special' people. You'll probably be a successful person someday…as long as a bicycle is not involved." They never said that and I'm grateful.

Riding a bike is one of the strangest experiences on the planet. It's a physics lesson on two wheels. The balance and the timing seem to make no sense. You can't do it…until you can do it. There's no other way to explain it. My family continued cheering me on and one day I finally did it.

My own bike memories have been re-visited this week as I've watched my 7-year-old struggle with the same scrapes and scratches. There's no doubt that the bruised ego has been the most painful injury sustained. A few days ago he said, "I just CAN'T do it! Bikes are stupid anyway." Yeah. I remember. Despite the growing frustration and the fact that bikes are stupid, my little guy kept climbing on that bike day after day. Something inside of him just wouldn't give up.

Yesterday he pushed the bike to the top of a hill in our massive front yard. His knees were scratched and his heart was heavy. I saw determination mixed with trepidation on his pale and solemn face. Then it happened. A miracle of physics. That bike came roaring down the hill straight as an arrow and as balanced as if Lance Armstrong were guiding it himself. My son's face lit up like the Christmas tree in Rockefeller Center. "I'm doing it! I'm doing it!" There was a radiant joy running through every inch of his 45 pound body. He glowed as he smoothly descended that hill keeping balance with all of nature. Any observer could tell it was the "rush of his life." He pedaled and pedaled...finally ending in a great crash near the front porch. But the crash had no bearing on him. The success of that awesome ride was the only emotion that hung in the air. We stood and cheered at the top of our lungs. Looking into his face, I wanted to cry. He hadn't given up. From this day on, he would be a bike rider.

My son's bicycle story is a commentary on a much deeper truth that will follow him the rest of his life. He dreamed of riding a bicycle. But in the middle of the struggle, the dream seemed like a nightmare. Long hours. Failures. Scratches and bruises. Then there was the decision. Would he get back on or accept defeat? He was tempted to throw in the towel. After all, bicycles are stupid. But the cheering crowd never lost faith in him. Finally, the decision was made to try again. The tenacity paid off...and when it did, there was the rush of achievement. It wasn't a rush based on talent or ability. No. Something far greater. Perseverance.

I'm glad my son got back on that bike. As he grows into a man, there will be times when his dreams seem utterly unreachable. He may even be tempted to look at his scratches and bruises...and walk away. But I hope he doesn't. I hope he looks back and remembers the hill in our front yard, the support of the cheering crowd, and the rush of the down-hill ride.

I Threw It Away

I did it. All of you parents out there have done it at one time or another. But few will openly admit it. Today I come clean. I threw some of my boys' artwork away. I threw it away. Yes, in the trash can. No, I didn't set it aside in a special box marked "Boys' Artwork Treasures." I hid the pile of papers in the kitchen trash can underneath the milk jug and the empty cracker box and, when no one was looking, I took the trash bag and deposited it in the big trash can outside. Yes, it will be picked up on Thursday. Yes, it will end up in a landfill with broken washing machines and junk mail. Shun me in the carpool line, if you must. But I know I'm not alone. In fact, in a moment of vulnerability, a well-respected local mom admitted to me that she sometimes sneaks her children's artwork and school papers into an empty cereal box and deposits the box into the trash can when no one is looking. You know who you are. Go public, Girlfriend. Live free.

Here's the truth that no red-blooded American parent wants to openly admit in the public square. Not everything my child creates with a dull red crayon and a cotton ball is worth saving. There. I said it. Not every Bible School craft project made with crooked Popsicle sticks and glitter should be in a museum. Not every school project with a check plus and a "Wow!" scribbled on it is worth treasuring for multiple generations to come. Just because my boys finger-painted it on the front porch doesn't mean it should be hanging in the Sistine Chapel. And incidentally, macaroni and felt scraps glued together on an average Saturday morning does not have to be hung on the refrigerator as though my child just discovered Antarctica. As long as there is room in the kitchen trash under the empty tuna can and the Diet Coke bottle, it can all be just a beautiful memory.

The way I see it, I'm doing my boys a tremendous favor by being moderate in what I choose to keep and treasure. Disposing of the "lesser" creations gives more prominence to the few that are kept. Plus, I'm helping them realize that everything they do is not brilliant and exceptional. Why is this important? I hope to save my boys from the following scenario once they get to college.

College Student: How could I get a C on this term paper?

Dr. Smith: The grammar was poor. The theme needed better development and your descriptive language was average, at best.

College Student: But, how can that be? I thought everything I touched was exceptional. I thought I was brilliant in every way. I'm certain my mom would hang this term paper on the refrigerator and use words like, "Way to go! You're something! Excellent effort!"

Dr. Smith: When your mom becomes your major professor, you'll be graduating with honors.

Whew! Join me in sparing our children that ill-fated scenario. I love our precious boys. I think they're smart and funny and talented. But everything they touch is not worth saving. That's just life. So come out of the closet, parents, and proudly take a stand. It's okay to throw it away. Really, it is. Now, I just have to figure a way to get rid of this newspaper before they come home from school.

A Climbing Wall and a Father's Love

My little boy looked small against the backdrop of the 20 ft. climbing wall. As he was strapped into the harness, he became deathly silent. I knew what he was thinking. He was wondering, "Can I do this? Is it too high? Am I strong enough?" Silence can mean a lot of things. Maybe he was just thinking, "I should have gone to the bathroom earlier." Either way, he looked scared. At the top of the climbing wall was a small gray button. When pushed, the button made a loud sound which announced to the waiting crowd, "This kid did it. He kept going. He made it to the top." My son wanted to push the button. But it meant going on the difficult journey.

He progressed well at first. The rocks were close together. He was able to navigate successfully. He wore a confident smile. About half-way up, the climb became more challenging. Rocks were further apart. It was harder to see what was above him. I could tell he was ready to give up. That's when the deep voice beside me spoke clearly, "Son, you can do it. There's a red rock right above your right foot. You can make it. There's a hand hold just above your left hand." Suddenly, a second wind blew into the little climber. And he kept going. He was nearing the top when it became even more difficult. His determined face looked worried. Confidence waned. Again, the voice, "Hey Buddy, you're almost there. You're so close. I know you can make it." In a matter of minutes, the gray button was pushed and the horn announced, "This kid made it to the top." His face glowed as he descended with the confidence that said, "I just scaled Mount Everest."

My son is in pretty good shape. He's a good climber. But I don't think that's why he made it to the top of the climbing wall. The well-timed words of encouragement spoken by his father gave him a distinctive edge.

If your dad guided you and affirmed you through life with love and support, call him and thank him. Better yet, write a letter. If you didn't receive the affirmation and blessing of your father, give heed to the following story.

My dad was two years old when he arrived at the Louisiana Methodist Orphanage in Northern Louisiana. His 4-year-old sister and 5-year-old brother accompanied him on the sidewalk as they began a journey which would last a lifetime. Their mom and dad had been killed in a car accident. They would forever be orphans. My dad and his siblings grew up at the orphanage and never experienced traditional "home life." He received the best the orphanage could offer. But he didn't get the personal attention of an intimate family life. He never heard the words, "Son, I know you can do it. I love you and I'm here for you." Despite his own personal loss, he became an excellent husband and a great dad to my brother and me. Key men stepped into his life at key points. His heavenly father embraced him with unconditional love and acceptance. I believe my dad made it to the top of the climbing wall. But it wasn't easy. Many people cheered him on his journey.

Some of you experienced a different kind of loss when it comes to fatherhood. Your dad was home every night. He lived in the same house. He stayed married to your mom. But you never experienced intimacy and affirmation. He never said, "I love you. I'm proud of you. I'm here for you if you've got questions about life." So you've spent a large part of your life trying to win the attention and affection of a man you barely know.

Maybe your dad failed your family morally. He left your mom for what seemed like "greater adventure" and in the process, he left you, too. He was busy. He had other items on his agenda that didn't involve parenting. To this day, he doesn't know the emotional havoc he's wreaked on your life. It looks like you "turned out alright" and people assume you must not have really needed a father's counsel or affirmation. You hesitate to admit that you did...and still do.

If your dad was less than a stellar supporter of you, learn to forgive. Ask God to fill in the empty spaces.

If you're a dad who has been "too busy" or if you haven't verbally supported your children, ask forgiveness. Whether your kids are 5 or 55, it's not too late. Admit your mistakes. Your children want to reach the top of the wall. And they need to know you're man enough to help them get there.

Endurance Training at Disney World

Forget training for the Boston Marathon. That's for wimps. If you really wanna know what you're made of, spend four days at Disney World. Yep, Disney training separates the men from the boys. It separates the women from the girls. An average of 78 miles of walking per day. And only the strong survive.

One morning last week, we awakened our boys and surprised them with a trip to Disney World. I know. Can you imagine? They woke up thinking it was an average day in Dresden and then, as though they had just won the Super Bowl, we said, "We're going to Disney World!" We sought fun-filled adventure and some serious family memory building. And we weren't disappointed.

Disney World is a plethora of material for a newspaper columnist. While I determined not to think about the column while vacationing, I couldn't help myself. Disney World is one great big study of human behavior. If you haven't taken the plunge to the World of Disney, I feel compelled to share my experiences and observations. Just call me your vacationing guru.

While my family had a truly wonderful and magical time, I want to warn you about three groups of people who experienced great suffering and human misery while at Disney World. Yes, believe it or not, even the happiest place on earth provided misery for a select few. Be warned, my friend. Be warned.

The first unfortunate group of Disney visitors- new parents. God bless these sweet naïve souls. They mistakenly believed their 9-month-old and 2-year-old needed to visit the great mouse. A grave error indeed. The 9-month-old was crying because he was hot and tired. The 2-year-old was crying because he was 2. The parents were crying because they had spent a cool $2000 to inflict this misery on their kids and themselves. And the visit to see the great mouse? Two quarters and the carousel horse at Kroger would have brought more joy to all. A word to the wise. If anyone in your party requires a pacifier, a stroller, or two daily naps, turn back. Turn back, I say.

The second group of suffering visitors-those who didn't seem to grasp the concept of "appropriate footwear." Those who couldn't forsake their girly girl high heel sandals or flip flops ended up paying a heavy price. And oh the price they paid. The bleeding blisters. The limping. The crying. Forsake your vanity, my friends. Only those shod with proper footwear live to see the finish line tape. When's the last time you saw marathoners running through Boston wearing palm tree flip flops? Point made.

I've saved the best group for last. Oh how I wanted to reach out and hug these brave souls. I wanted to give them Tylenol and energy drinks. I wanted to tell them I understood that it had all been a terrible mistake. I'm referring to those who were at the park chaperoning groups of middle school children. God bless them. God bless them every one. The wrinkled brows. The worried looks. The "Where's Brandon? And didn't you know Ashley wasn't supposed to ride roller coasters? Who has a paper bag?" Oh my. The stories are endless. These brave chaperones had volunteered for the job at a PTO meeting back in the fall. Come to think of it, the punch did smell a little funny that night. And now it was too late to turn back. Too late. I know. Some of you are thinking, "Well, I remember chaperoning Blake's choir trip to Disney in '94...and it was a magical experience." Yeah. That's what people say about having a baby…several years later. Time heals all wounds.

Our family had a grand vacation. We hugged the great mouse, rode the roller coasters, saw the sights, and lived to tell about it. If we could do it all again, we would jump at the chance. Just not tomorrow.

Vacuum Cleaners and Chia Pets

It was an average Saturday morning at our house. But instead of the typical Saturday morning cartoons, my boys were mesmerized by an infomercial about an amazing and talented vacuum cleaner. Based on the enthusiasm of the host and the audience, this machine could eliminate the evils of dust and dirt while bringing about world peace and fostering family harmony. It was an all-American lesson on creative marketing. And unfortunately, my naïve children bought it hook, line, and drapery attachment. The zealous host convinced them that their lives were in utter ruin because of the run-of-the-mill vacuum cleaner which was contaminating their home, their lives, and their hope for future happiness.

It was about 6:15 when two inspired little American males with chocolate milk mustaches and wrinkled Spiderman pajamas came running back to our bedroom. The planned sales pitch was memorized, "Mommy, Daddy, we've got to buy this! We just have to! It's amazing! You won't believe what it can do!" I wanted to say, "Look, if it's an invention that can keep kids from waking up at 6:00 on a Saturday morning, here's my credit card. Knock yourself out. Buy two." Instead, I managed to utter one word, "Huh?" "Mommy, this vacuum cleaner can keep you from getting sick. It can keep the furniture from getting dusty. It can make your life lots happier!" That's when it hit me. All trauma and difficulty that I or anyone else had ever experienced in life probably went back to an issue we had never even considered. We had subconsciously ignored the obvious …the power of the household vacuum cleaner.

I managed to verbalize a few words, "Look guys, we don't need a new vacuum cleaner. We have a perfectly good vacuum cleaner. None of us is sick. We're all happy. Since when are you two concerned about cleanliness? You both have dirty clothes under your beds, a moldy set of plastic dinosaurs in the bath tub, and there's a half-eaten grape Blow Pop stuck to your dresser. We're not about to buy a new vacuum cleaner."

"Mom, you don't understand what this vacuum cleaner can do. It's WAY better than the one we have! The one we have is not a good vacuum cleaner at all! THIS vacuum cleaner can go up stairs by itself!" "Boys, I hate to break it to you... We don't have stairs."

Marketing. It's an amazing thing. Two boys were easily convinced they needed a vacuum cleaner that could go up stairs. The fact that they lived in a house without stairs didn't even thwart their enthusiasm. That's the genius of marketing. All of us know that marketing and advertising are the keys to the American economy. Just look at the Chia Pet which was introduced in 1982. Most people in America today can sing the jingle, "Ch Ch Ch Ch-ia! Ch Ch Ch Ch-ia!" The catchy jingle convinced thousands of people that one thing was missing in their lives... a ceramic puppy covered in herb grass. What's not to love about that?

Is it any shock that the same company that came up with the Chia pet also invented the Clapper? Again, the commercial was the key, "Clap on! Clap off! Clap on! Clap off!" Americans began to realize that rising from a chair to turn off a light was just too taxing and aerobically challenging. Clapping loudly from the brown vinyl recliner was the way to go. When little Mary Louise played her piano recital music at Grandma's house, the applause made Grandma's living room look like a disco.

I'd like to enlighten my boys on resisting the powerful pull of commercials. They once told me I'd look younger and more beautiful if I bought the special hair care products available for only $19.99. ($34.00 with shipping and handling.) I just laughed. Poor guys. They really don't get it, do they? I would never spend that much valuable money on hair care. And besides, would new hair care products really make someone like me happy? Of course not. What were they thinking? A woman my age needs a Thigh Master, a bottle of Corti-Slim, and a set of Ginzu knives.

Chapter 3

Small Town Livin': The Gift that Keeps Givin'

What Can I Bring?

You just can't invite people for dinner anymore. People no longer possess the skill necessary to walk into your house and eat dinner at your table. No. They want to bring something. They HAVE to bring something. They must be carrying something in their hands when they cross the threshold of your home or it produces global warming or some other alarming calamity.

This agonizing process starts with a simple phone conversation. "Hey Gloria, can you and your family come eat dinner with us Friday night?"

"Friday night? Yes, we're free. What can I bring?"

"Just bring yourselves. Is 6:00 okay?"

"Yes, 6:00 is fine. I'll bring a salad and some rolls."

"No. Just bring yourselves."

"Great. We'll look forward to it. I'll just bring dessert and some sliced tomatoes then."

"Gloria, don't worry about bringing anything. Really. Just come."

"Thanks for inviting us. We look forward to it. I'll just bring a watermelon and a cantaloupe."

"Is there a problem with the phone line, Gloria? I already have plans for a mandarin orange fruit salad. So, don't worry about the watermelon and cantaloupe. Just come."

"Yes, we'll be glad to come. I'll just bring paper plates, napkins, and some of those silly straws the kids love!"

"Don't worry about the plates or the silly straws, Gloria. Just come at 6:00."

"Oh, alright. Remember when my Aunt Bonnie went through that baking frenzy in the fall of '99? I still have two loaves of her famous banana bread in the deep freeze out in the shed. 'Bonnie's Bodacious Banana Bread' won a blue ribbon at the county fair that year. I'll just thaw both loaves and bring a stick of butter."

At this point in the conversation, I'm ready for a tall glass of lemonade and a foot massage. Then came the solution.

"Gloria, let's start over, shall we?"

"Okay. Go ahead."

"Gloria, can you and your family come for dinner Friday night?"

"Sure! What can I bring?"

"Well, I was wondering if you could bring a pot roast? And some new potatoes cooked in the crock pot? I've been hankerin' for chocolate if you feel like baking some brownies. Of course, we'll need something to drink. How about making some fresh lemonade? We like to eat on real plates, so, if you wanted to bring your china and a freshly ironed tablecloth, we'd just love it! The bathrooms will need to be cleaned and the front porch will need to be swept. So, if you could come an hour early, it would help me greatly. Would you mind dropping by the Farmer's Market on the way to pick up some cucumbers and sweet corn? Also, could you run by the dry cleaner and pick up my green jacket? My son has been struggling with learning his multiplication tables. After scrubbing the toilet in the guest bathroom, would you mind doing flash cards with him? The cats need to be fed. The dogs need to have their water bowls scrubbed. Oh, and a loaf of your homemade garlic bread would make the evening just sing!"

A Grand Opening and a Tractor Pull

Sometimes life is just too sweet. Too much excitement for the small-town soul. Such was my experience last week when, within a 24 hour period, I experienced a grand opening and a tractor pull. It started out as an average day at the Smartt household. Up early. Breakfast with the kids. Off to school. That was the end of "average."

I'm a pretty social person. I like parties. I like waving to people when we pass on the road. I like the fact that people in West Tennessee talk to you even when they don't know you. That's probably one of my favorite things about small-town life. As a middle-aged, small-town party person, I knew I had to be at the grand opening of our new Wal-Mart. It would be a time to visit with friends and neighbors and search the aisles for a newspaper column. West Tennesseans rarely disappoint.

The party with friends and neighbors that morning was such fun and brought to mind a classic small-town story. One day a friend from a large metropolitan city was with me in a small-town retail facility. She held up two sweaters for me to examine. Her words were simple, "Which looks better? The green or the blue?"

Just about that time, an older lady approached my friend and said quite passionately, "Oh, Girl, that green really brings out your eyes. The blue doesn't do a thing for you!"

I turned to the woman and said, "I heartily agree! And can you believe these lovely sweaters are on sale?"

She replied, "I know, Girl! What a deal! I was thinking of buying one for my granddaughter. You think a teenager would like these?"

I responded enthusiastically, "Oh absolutely! Did you see the purple ones up against the wall? Let's go look and see if they have her size."

After a few minutes of enjoyable small-town banter, the older woman went to the check-out and I turned back to my friend who said, "Who was that, Lisa?"

"I have no idea."

That's when the eyes of my big-city friend grew to the size of turkey platters. "WHAT? What do you mean, 'I have no idea.' You're telling me you don't even KNOW that woman."

"Yes, that's what I'm telling you."

"Well then, why did she just come up to us like she knew us?"

"Didn't you hear what she said? The green really brings out your eyes and the blue doesn't do a thing for you! That's why she came up to us. She was helping you look your best, Girlfriend!"

My friend smiled and shook her head.

The evening of the retail store grand opening, my family and I made a trip to the Obion County Fair. That's where we experienced the tractor pull. My, my, my! A trip to the moon would have been no more exciting for my two boys. The unrelenting noise. The raw mechanical power. The overalls-clad crowd cheering for their friends and neighbors. At one point, I looked at my two smiling boys. Cotton candy and caramel apple residue were clinging to their dust-covered faces. And that's when I knew. Just like the green sweater on my friend, small-town life was the perfect fit.

An Auction is My Kind of Bargain

There's nothing like a good southern auction. During the last year, my family and I have been privileged to go to some wonderful auctions here in West Tennessee. It's been a rewarding and fun experience every time. For those of you who've never been to local auctions, allow me to give you some auction rules.

The first rule is that your kids are going to need $10 each for concessions. Nobody's hungry until they smell the burgers and hot dogs.....and see all the other fortunate kids carrying around bags of chips bought at the concession stand. To combat this kind of peer pressure the following speech should be delivered to your children as soon as you get to the auction: "Look, you can't be really hungry. It's only 10:15 in the morning. That kid with a double cheeseburger, Cheetos, and a super-sized Coke is probably here with his grandma." (When a child comes to an auction with Grandma, it's likely they'll be hitting the concession stand a little earlier and a little more frequently than children who are at an auction with regular parents.)

The second rule of an auction is that you need to keep your children with you at all times. If they wander off, be careful how you gesture for them to come to you. One angry hand wave and you can unknowingly end up with a set of ceramic unicorns. "One man's trash is another man's treasure." If you don't believe it, go to an auction.

The third rule is that you need to find an older, tastefully-dressed woman to sit by. She'll help you know what's worth something and what's not. I know nothing about glassware, china patterns, or antique furniture. When I say I know nothing about them, I mean **nothing**. I went to an auction once where I saw a lovely little dresser I wanted to buy. I decided I would loosen the ole' wallet and be willing to lay over a cool $100 for said item. It sold for over $1,000. When I looked with amazement at my tastefully-dressed friend, she whispered in my ear, "Darlin', that's over 100 years old." Oh. I had no clue. I thought it was cool that down near the floor there was a little mirror on the dresser. I was told the mirror was designed to see if the petticoats were straight. Okay. I'll not be applying for a job at an antique store. I saw a pretty little green bowl that would be perfect for my homemade mashed potatoes. It went for $85 and I bet the person who bought it won't even give that sweet little bowl the privilege of serving up a mound of mashed taters. Too bad, really.

The fourth and final rule is the hardest one to follow. Don't get too caught up in the competitive nature of the beast. An auction comes alive when two competitive participants enjoy a friendly bidding war over the Santa Claus soup bowls or the brass elephant set. Not getting caught up in the competition of the event is particularly hard for my type A son. He said, "Oh, Mom, if you had kept holding your hand up, you would have WON that!!" Yeah. I would have won it alright. I would have ended up paying $18 for the squirrel salt and pepper shakers. Even a novice like me knows that squirrel salt and pepper shakers aren't worth more than $17.

Auctions are a wonderful learning experience. Where else can your kids learn math, capitalism, and patience all in the same day? The fact that all those lessons can be served up with a burger and a dill pickle….well, that's just icing on the cake.

Three Cheers for Local Politics

Some of you believe that a columnist who writes about cat therapists, garage sales, and a fear of lawnmowers doesn't know anything about politics. Au contraire, my friend. Au contraire. It was 1970 when I first became a part of the political process. The experience will be forever etched in my memory.

The scene begins in a tiny town in West Kentucky. My parents had gathered around the kitchen table with some friends talking until two o'clock in the morning. All four had determined that some progressive changes needed to be made on the local school board. The other couple had six children in the system. Mom and Dad had two. They all agreed that one of them would have to run for the school board. It was determined that because my parents were both educators, one of them should be the candidate. My dad is one of the most vivacious, engaging individuals you could ever hope to meet. But, let's just say he's a little too outspoken. A mild description. Mom was the clear candidate.

We all worked hard on the campaign trail which led through a small town and the surrounding rural countryside of West Kentucky. We made home visits explaining our "vision for change." We wrote "Vote for Regina Golden" on little note pads and handed them out to voters. Election Day came. Mom cooked a big breakfast, as always, and said, "It will all be fine no matter what. We gave it our best." And it was fine. Mom lost by only 25 votes.

Change on the school board didn't happen. Everything stayed the same. Within one year, my parents moved us out of that town into a community they believed had a more progressive vision for education.

That was my first lesson in local politics. It was so much hard work and in the end, through the eyes of a second grader, it had all been a terrible waste. Now, through the eyes of a 42-year-old, it wasn't a waste at all. No. Our entire family had become a part of the process. An honorable, visionary process which makes this country great.

Political races are gearing up all over West Tennessee now. Signs are emerging. Stories are being written about the candidates. You can almost smell the glorious process brewing, like a pot of fresh coffee.

As a recent transplant to Northwest Tennessee, I'm at a great advantage or disadvantage depending upon how you look at it. When I read about the candidates or meet them in person, I've no idea who their daddy is or who their cousin married or what foolish thing they did back in the 70's. No. I've no idea who they may have offended at the pancake breakfast in '89 or what they did at the city council meeting the year all heck broke loose. Everyone has a clean slate with me. Each candidate stands on his or her own two feet. I think I'm at an advantage.

Candidates, you can be assured I hold nothing from your past against you. I don't know your past. I'm interested in your future. I'm listening for your vision, your ideas, your goals. Competitive debate and disagreement are expected. Mud slinging is an absolute no no. I'm sure I don't even have to write that. Most of your mamas taught you that concept long before this Texas Transplant became a newspaper columnist.

Months from now when all the elections are over, I wish for each winning candidate a proper dose of appreciation and humility. And for those who come up a few votes short, I pray they will have the incredible class and dignity of a woman I witnessed in 1970. Win or lose, small children are watching.

Make Room for Flamingoes

I like pink plastic yard flamingoes. I'm serious. I love a town that has room for self- expression. For those of you who have the pink flamingoes, let me warn you. Some people will try to tell you they're tacky. Don't listen. The same people who think the flamingoes are tacky just painted the inside of their house olive green and mocha. Go figure. A few years ago, these same people thought olive green and mocha were atrocious colors. Critical people are fickle. They can't be trusted.

I like the fact that I live in a town that has room for yard flamingoes. America is changing in that regard. The area we moved from in Texas was starting to take an ugly turn concerning self-expression. Several friends lived in neighborhoods in Houston that forbid the presence of children's bikes in the driveway or front yard. Some areas wouldn't allow even a small camper to be parked in the drive. Some of my friends couldn't put a storage shed in their backyard. How could someone find my house if the bikes couldn't be in the yard? It's part of the directions to our home. "Turn left on Cleveland. When you see yellow Tonka trucks, plastic army men, Jedi light sabers, and two bikes that look like they've been in a dog fight, that's our house."

I'm glad I live in a small town in West Tennessee. I'm glad that among the beautiful azaleas and dogwoods, live real people. I'm glad some people paint the inside of their houses trendy colors. I'm glad others keep theirs the same. That's called "community."

I once saw a TV report on a neighborhood in Florida. That neighborhood had extreme community rules which caused every house to look exactly alike. I don't want to live in a neighborhood where every house looks exactly alike. I don't even want to live in a neighborhood where all the houses cost the same. You know the neighborhoods I'm talking about. "Welcome to Rich Rolling Rivers. We sell houses in the $190's." Don't dare come in and build a $187,000 house. It would send our property value plummeting. If you want to build a $187,000 house...go find a neighborhood that has houses in the 180's.

I know. Excessive "community rule writing" is done in the name of protecting the re-sale value or preserving property value. I just don't remember this being an issue when I was growing up. We lived in a beautiful neighborhood. But I don't remember my parents pulling their hair out at night worrying if the rusty bike parked next door was going to cost them money on re-sale. They were concerned about loving the people in our neighborhood. They forgot to be concerned about property value.

Before you send an e-mail telling me about your neighbor who has five old cars up on blocks, hasn't mowed his grass in two years, and has a pit bull running loose in the front yard; let me clarify what I'm saying here. There are some things that are just included in general neighborhood courtesies. Mowing is one of those courtesies. Keeping dogs peacefully restrained is a courtesy. Keeping most of what's in the driveway drivable is a courtesy. But, let's not forget to give people room for self-expression. Let's leave space for a flamingo now and then. I think we're even broad-minded enough for an occasional yard dwarf, don't you?

How Big is a Small Town?

There's some confusion out there in the general population of America. Not everyone knows what a small town is. We moved here from a community in Texas with a population of 125,000. Sometimes people would move to that community and say, "This is the first time I've ever lived in a small town."

I didn't criticize their obviously narrow view of the world. I'd just smile and say, "This is not a small town. I could take you to some small towns. Trust me. After the trip, you'd know the difference. Any town where you can get a fat-free mocha latte at 1:00 a.m. is NOT small. If there's a Target, an Outback Steakhouse, and a Starbucks complete with 24-hour laundry facilities, you're not exactly in the backwoods.

My husband grew up in a town that was so small it wasn't even a town. Some of you know what I mean. It's an unincorporated little section of the globe. Do any of you know where Northcutts Cove is? It's in middle Tennessee near Altamont. People in Northcutts Cove and Altamont know what a small town is. In a small town you not only know all the people, but you can identify every dog as well. "Look, there's ole' Jim Smith's coon dog, Rascal. He's on the trail of somethin' in Aunt Lydia's back 40." Yeah. That's a small town.

When you drive through a small town and decide to eat at the ever popular, "Miss Lucy's Diner/Gas Station/Grocery Store/Post Office," it's not a good idea to ask for a fat-free mocha latte. On the other hand, if you go to Starbucks, don't expect a piece of lemon meringue pie that will bring tears of joy to your eyes. Starbucks serves biscotti. I've had biscotti. It's a stale crunchy reminder of how good a piece of homemade pie would be.

My big-city friend was once traveling and stopped to eat lunch at a small-town diner. The homemade pie was so good that she decided to buy a few pies to take home. (This is a true story, mind you.) When paying her tab, my friend had this conversation with the lady at the counter:
"I would like some pie to take home."

"Why sure, Honey, what piece would you like?"

"Well, I'd like to buy two whole pies."

"Oh Honey, I can't sell you two pies."

"I'll give you $25 per pie. I'll take a lemon and a chocolate."

"No, Hon, you don't understand what I'm sayin'. I can't sell you two whole pies because the construction boys will be in soon and that might cause me to run short. They count on a piece of homemade pie every day. I wouldn't want to disappoint them."

Ding Ding Ding…10 points for a small town. My bet is that Starbucks would sell you the table and chairs if you offered them the right price. Not that lady. She had loyal small-town customers. They counted on her.

I'm not making a judgment call about whether big-city life or small-town life is better. I've enjoyed both. I don't mind admitting I like a good latte now and then. A mall is a nice convenience occasionally. There's a lot to be said for the diversity of larger communities.

But I'll be honest. I'm kind of fond of a little place in the woods outside a medium town called Dresden. It has a front porch and lots of trees. It's not exactly what most people would consider a "cosmopolitan" place. But being on the cover of Cosmo was never one of my life goals. If I remember correctly, my goals included loving God, spending time with my wonderful husband, watching my boys play, and encouraging people. I'd like to eventually become an excellent writer. I think small-town life will suit those aspirations just fine. And if I never eat biscotti again, I'll consider myself all the richer.

I Love a Small Town Parade

I enjoy the Macy's Thanksgiving Day Parade on television every year. How often do you get to see a famous Broadway performer singing next to a Garfield the size of a parking garage? When else do you get to see elaborate floats that look like mini-Disney Worlds flowing effortlessly down the streets of New York City? The emcees are usually famous movie or TV stars dressed in designer coats and ridiculous-looking hats. They pretend they're freezing to death, but we never feel sorry for them. They make more money in 11 minutes than the rest of us make in a year. And if they had any sense, they'd have gotten some long underwear from Rural King and eliminated the shivering and shaking.

As endearing as the Macy's Thanksgiving Day Parade may be, it can't compare to a small town parade. You'll not find a Snoopy the size of New Hampshire in most small town parades. Small town parades rarely have Broadway performers or nationally-famous emcees. They have something far better. It's something that Macy's will never be able to buy or replicate. It's the comments that can be heard only at a small town parade.

Here are a few of those comments:

"Uncle George, throw me some Laffy Taffy!"

"Louise, your 3-legged dog looks cute dressed like the Lion King."

"In the Scooby-Doo costume, is that Mabel from the coffee shop?"

"Here comes the fire truck. Wave at Jim and he'll throw more candy."

"Mrs. Smith, I didn't know you could drive a John Deere!"

"I can't believe little Clarinda grew up to be the Homecoming Queen. Remember when she was too shy to even look you in the face?"

"Troop 78 really outdid themselves this year. Who'd have thought you could make palm trees out of paper towel rolls?"

"The high school band sounds good. Joleen, get in step, Sweetheart! Daddy's using the video camera!"

"That's not Rupert Henderson on the high school football float, is it? I remember when he was knee-high to a grasshopper."

"Bobby Joe, slow down that convertible, young man!! Little Miss Turnip Greens is holding on for dear life back there!"

Such is life in small town America. Some people in the world might find small town parades backward or less exciting than parades in the big city. I couldn't disagree more. It takes time to appreciate the artful way small towns function. I'll admit that when we first moved here, it took some adjusting. Some days I wasn't so sure about living in a small town. But the people of this community encouraged us and supported us. Dear friends here reminded us to focus on the positive.

Our family was blessed to be at the Soybean Festival Parade this year. The sense of community put a smile on my face. Even though I'm a newcomer, I saw several people I knew and I got the strange sensation that I was home. The slow pace didn't bother me. It was refreshing and engaging.

This is the time of year our community has the opportunity to welcome newcomers to the area. Having been here only a year myself, I have some advice to give the new residents. A newcomer must be willing to be an initial observer and student rather than a skeptic and critic. Don't waste time focusing on what we don't have. Instead, take the time to discover the riches of what we do have.

Chapter 4

Holidays: Enough Said

Need a Valentine's Day Do-Over?

Valentine's Day is over. It's done. Finished. But there's no need for despair. I'm offering you a second chance. Some of you married folk just need a "Do-Over." Who needs a second chance? Take the quiz and find out. There's a separate quiz for men and women.

The "Did I Mess Up on Valentine's Day?" POP QUIZ for Men:

1. When I arrived home from work on Valentine's Day, I said:

a. Honey, I'm home! The babysitter will be here in an hour. We have reservations. I'll watch the kids while you get ready. But, trust me, you're already beautiful. I'll also find a vase for this beautiful array of flowers I brought to express my undying love!

b. Honey, I'm home! I love you! Happy Valentine's Day! What's for supper?

c. Honey, I'm home! I love you! Happy Valentine's Day! The mold needs to be cleaned out of my thermos. What's for supper?

d. Honey, I'm home! The mold needs to be cleaned out of my thermos. What's for supper?

2. The card I got for the love of my life said:

a. If I had the chance to live my life again, there might be things I would change. But the one thing I would do again, in a heartbeat, is marry you. Your love has been the best thing that has ever happened to me. I owe you my life.....and you have it. In Love for a Lifetime, your grateful husband.

b.   On a Post-It note from work: I love you.   Happy Valentine's Day!

c.   On a Post-It note from work: I love you.   Happy Valentine's Day!   Did you get a chance to pay the car insurance bill?

d. What card? Was I supposed to get a card?

The "Did I Mess Up on Valentine's Day?" POP QUIZ for Women:

1. When I woke up on Valentine's Day morning, I said:

a. I love you. You will forever be my valentine...and I have big plans for tonight.

b. I love you. You will forever be my valentine....but your snoring kept me up most of the night.

c. I love you. You will forever be my valentine...but your snoring kept me up most of the night. And by the way, your breath stinks.

d. You snored. Your breath stinks. And I'm in a rush. Can you make breakfast?

2. When my husband called me during the day on Valentine's Day, I said:

a. I love you. I miss you. I can't wait to see you.

b. I love you. Remember to pick up dog food on your way home from work.

c. I love you. Remember to pick up dog food **and** mouthwash on your way home from work.

d. Remember to pick up dog food and mouthwash on your way home from work. I'm sleeping in the guest room tonight. I can't take the snoring.

I don't really have to "break it down" for you, do I? No, I didn't think so. For some of you, the "Did I mess up on Valentine's Day?" pop quiz hurt a little. That's good. Pain can be an incredible motivator. But be not discouraged. All is not lost. Make reservations. Make plans. Look your valentine square in the eyes and say, "I need a second chance." (Don't forget to use a breath mint first.)

Easter Sunday Amidst the Rubble

Like all of you, I've been absolutely grieved for the families who have experienced such devastation and loss during the recent tornadoes. One picture keeps coming to mind. The picture of a man sitting in a recliner in the midst of utter chaos and rubble. The weathered recliner seemed the only item left of his home and belongings. And he was just sitting there amidst the wreckage. What was going through his mind? It was all gone. The beginning of a new life would be a difficult one. But, for those who've lost dear and precious family members, difficult is a horrible understatement. Our words become completely inadequate. The precious people who were killed in the recent tornadoes are irreplaceable. For some of you, there will always be an empty space at Christmas dinner. A shedding of tears at Thanksgiving. To all of you whose lives were changed in April, 2006, we grieve with you. To all of you who will never forget the tragic phone call bearing the bad news, we reach out our arms and say a pitifully inadequate, "I'm sorry."

When my dad was on a volunteer work mission in Florida after Hurricane Andrew, he witnessed miles and miles of complete destruction. Mounds of devastation. The hurricane had laid waste to it all and at times, the feeling was hopeless. But in between the rubble, he could sometimes see small shoots of green. New life. A reminder that all was not lost. God wasn't finished with us yet.

West Tennessee has been hit hard. Loss of life. Loss of property. And in the midst of the grief and rubble, we celebrate Easter. We celebrate Christ's sacrifice and glorious resurrection. We celebrate the fact that this dark and difficult world is not our real home. No. We await a far better world. Not long ago, we were talking about heaven at our house. My husband and I said that it's hard to describe how long we'll be in heaven. Billions of years would only be the beginning. My younger son said, "Trillions of years." We said, "Trillions and trillions of years." My older son said with a smile and an air of finality, "Infinity." Yes, infinity. A glorious truth.

When I was a little girl, we awoke while it was still dark and went to the Easter Sunrise service every year. Usually held outdoors, it always seemed cold, dark, damp. Everyone was quiet. Somber. We stood around in a huddled circle, trying to stay warm. And then it happened. Orange and red peeking over the horizon. A warm glow. A reminder that the cold and darkness of this current world had been overcome. The Son of God had brought warmth and light. He had paid the price for our sin and offered permanent forgiveness and mercy. I will always remember my dad's deep voice singing, "Up from the grave He arose. He arose a victor from the dark domain. And He lives forever with His saints to reign. He arose. He arose. Hallelujah. Christ arose." And the good news continues to spring up like shoots of green in the midst of a dark and confusing world.

Weddings, Weddings, Weddings

It's almost June and love is in the air. Welcome to "Wedding Season." Somewhere in America today a bride is trying to convince a groom that wearing a mauve cummerbund doesn't threaten his masculine image. Somewhere in this great country of ours, a bride and her mom are at a bakery analyzing data to determine whether they want the butter cream icing or the apricot filling. The expressions on their faces would indicate that they're settling a matter of national security.

Sometimes perfectly normal people lose all sense of reality when called upon to plan a wedding. While visiting the over-priced caterer, the bride's mom starts crying because she doesn't like the shrimp puffs. The bride starts crying because she can't believe her mom doesn't like the shrimp puffs. The bride, on the other hand, loves the shrimp puffs. In fact, she declares loudly that she has always DREAMED of having the shrimp puffs at her wedding and she doesn't know if she can go on with her life…without the shrimp puffs. Dad starts crying because he doesn't want to pay for the shrimp puffs. The bride starts wailing because she thinks Dad's not being supportive of her "dream" to serve the shrimp puffs. See what I mean? These are probably normal people. They've just been possessed by the "wedding demon." Poor things. Someone needs to splash cold water on their faces until they come to their senses.

I admit it. I'm sympathetic toward the groom. He has to invest six months of his life hugging the bride saying, "It's okay, Honey. Really. It will be okay." What he wants to say is, "What in the heck are we doing? Run by the grocery store and pick up a chocolate cake and meet me in your grandma's backyard in two hours. I'll bring the minister and my parents. That should do it." I think the groom has a point.

Let's be honest. Some weddings have gotten out of hand. Big-city businesses have learned to market their extravagant wedding services with just one little question to the engaged couple, "Don't you want to remember this day forever?" Okay. I don't get that question. I have never heard a human being say, "Honey, did we get married in St. Louis or San Diego? I always forget. Was it at a church or on the beach? Ever since we decided not to go with that opulent floral/catering package, the day is all just a blur." Let's get real. Even if you got married on a Tuesday morning right after mowing the front yard, wouldn't you still REMEMBER the day you pledged your life-long love to another human being? Yeah. I thought so.

Our wedding was simple. We had lots of special music, a message by a dear friend, prayers and vows, cake and punch. Friends and relatives came from all over the country to celebrate with us. We could have never afforded shrimp puffs. Somehow we've managed to stay married for 17 years even though the cruel circumstances of life denied us the shrimp puffs. Amazing.

At the rehearsal, my mom stood up and said with a smile, "Everyone, just relax about tomorrow. If they walk out of here married, it will have been a great success." I appreciated her attitude. It's in great contrast with a story my friend tells about a wedding she was in recently. She got a drink from the water fountain shortly before the ceremony. A little bit of water spilled on her bridesmaid dress and the bride's mom went ballistic. She started yelling and crying, saying it would ruin the pictures. Someone needed to step in and say, "Mom, go eat a shrimp puff. Eat all the shrimp puffs. In fact, station yourself at the shrimp puff table and we'll meet you there later." The poor lady couldn't see the forest for the trees.

I have a novel idea. When a young couple gets their marriage license, I think they should be assigned an all-day interview with a couple who has been married more than 50 years. This might shed some valuable light on the institution of marriage. It might help them clarify some things about the wedding, too. When you read about weddings from the past, it seems they were much simpler. "She wore a lovely tan suit and the wedding took place in her parents' front yard. They shared cake and punch with friends and relatives on the back porch." My guess is that the planning for the whole event took only a few hours. Maybe the focus was on the marriage and not as much on the wedding.

There's nothing wrong with a lovely or even opulent wedding. I have no problem with shrimp puffs. Shrimp is a perfectly delightful food. My only recommendation is that young couples focus as much time planning the marriage as they do planning the wedding. A wedding is one day. A marriage is forever.

Costume Conflicts

It happens every year. Costume time. Time to decide what my boys (7 and 9) are going to "be." Costume time brings out the left brain/right brain conflict in every family in America. Everything inside my being says, "Let's be something no one else has even thought of. Let's be creative. Let's operate 'outside the box' and come up with something truly original." It was time for a meeting of the minds. Here are a few of the ideas I recently presented to my boys on an average Saturday afternoon:

"Hey guys, if you'll let me cover you in wet clay and let it dry....you'd be ant mounds!! I could even get little plastic ants and super glue them to the sides. Wouldn't that just be delightful?" They both frowned.

"Boys, we could totally cover you in cotton balls and you'd be a real snow drift or a snowman." They both frowned.

"I know! I could wrap your body in cardboard, put lots of fluffy pink insulation on your head.....and you'd be a snow cone! Wouldn't that be COOL?" Again, frowns.

"I've got it!! We'll starch your hair and clothing to make it look like you're in a wind storm. We could call you, 'Wind Men.'" Wrinkled brows and question mark glances.

"Here's one! You could each wear a brown sweat suit. We could staple fall leaves all over you. We could make a big headpiece of branches and leaves. We could even put a REAL nest on your head! Haven't you always dreamed of being a TREE?"

Their reply, "Not really."

And then there was silence. Deafening silence. I began to shuffle my feet a little. The boys gazed out the window. It was clear we were at a stand still. Where is Dr. Phil when you need him? It's costume time and a mediator is in order. My articulate older son hesitantly became the spokesperson for both boys. He stepped forward and cleared his throat.

"Mom, well, y'see, we really don't want to put insulation on our heads or starch our hair or wear a bird's nest. No offense, of course. Uh, well, we already know what we want to be this year. I want to be Darth Vader and Jonathan wants to be Batman. And Mom…uh, we want to just buy the suits at Wal-Mart." It's a good thing I was sitting down.

Again, silence. A large imaginary rock of disappointment had fallen from the sky and plunged me into the hardwood floor of our living room. The bizarre truth kept running through my mind…My kids want to be "normal." I was prepared for the rigors of parenting. I knew it wouldn't be easy. But, I never expected kids who wanted to be "normal." I gave them each a hug and said with a courageous smile, "Well, alrighty then. Looks like we've come to a decision. Darth Vader and Batman it is."

One of the first lessons of parenting is to learn what hills are worth dying on. Learn to let go of certain expectations. Okay. My boys want to join a myriad of boys their age in wearing polyester costumes honoring fictitious movie characters. They don't want to utilize my creativity. They don't want to stand out in the crowd. I can learn to live with that. Life marches on.

So, if you see us on Halloween night, you'll see two adorable little boys dressed in Darth Vader and Batman costumes, complete with light saber and batarang. They'll not stand out.

They'll look quite normal. Their dad, dressed in jeans and a flannel shirt, will be carrying the flashlight. And if you see a fat 6ft. snow cone walking next to them, well…that's just pure coincidence.

Halloween Candy Conspiracy

There's a conspiracy in America. I wouldn't be able to sleep at night if I didn't warn all readers out there. It's called the "Halloween Candy Conspiracy." Buyer beware.

The conspiracy unfolds in early September. Aisles and aisles of Halloween candy surface in every major retail outlet. Wait! Isn't it a bit early to be selling Halloween candy? Oh no. It's all part of the twisted little plan the conspirators use to snare innocent shoppers into a whirlwind of irrational, caffeine-induced shopping behavior. It starts with a sign that proclaims, "SALE! STOCK UP NOW! Was: $3.69. Now: $2.99." Seeing the sale sign, one immediately says, "Gosh, I better grab a few bags of Snickers and M&M's. I'd hate to be caught off guard in eight weeks when I'll actually be needing the candy for trick-or-treaters or school parties." People from all walks of life naively take home four bags of candy on a typical Saturday afternoon in early September. They put it on the top shelf of the pantry. Everything is fine....fine until the next day at about 4:30 p.m. Then it hits. It's that horrible I-have-to-have-chocolate yearning. I'm convinced there are times a woman would sell her car for a Hershey bar......but, of course, that's not necessary. Thanks to the Halloween candy sale, there's a luring sound coming from the pantry door. Sure. She could eat a banana. It would be so simple. But no. The poor woman snatches the Snickers bag from the pantry shelf. It's all over but the crying.

A week later the same shopper is back at the local retail outlet. All four bags of candy purchased last week are gone and the shopper is determined to buy nothing but the absolute necessities. But there it is. Aisles and aisles of chocolate candy. This time it's no longer $2.99/bag. Oh no. The conspirators have it marked down to $2.50. A huge sign reminds every shopper, "IT WON'T LAST!" What an understatement.

Determined to get a good deal on Halloween candy, the naive shopper once again buys the candy. This time there is pure determination in her eyes. She hides the bags high above the towels and toilet paper in the guest bathroom closet. She is determined not to get within ten feet of the candy until the first doorbell ring on Oct. 31st. Day one passes. No transgression. Day two passes with no problem. On day three the devious little kids say, "Mom, can't we have just one piece of the Halloween candy?"

Resolve crumbles. She innocently says, "Gee, it won't hurt to give them just a piece or two, will it?" Let's see. I'll just open a bag of the M&M's. Within four days, all candy is a mere memory.

Our naive friend returns once again to the retail outlet. This time she decides to walk in and head straight for the light bulb aisle. She won't get near the candy. As she walks through the parking lot she says under her breath, "I'll just pass out kiwi fruit to all the neighborhood kids. What kid doesn't love kiwi?" When she walks in the front door, she is hit in the face by a large shelf of chocolate candy positioned right by the entrance. A sign the size of Delaware proclaims, "Candy Sale. $1.50/bag. BARGAIN! BARGAIN! BARGAIN!"

Does our shopper see the sign and flee? Oh no. She says aloud, "Gee! $1.50/bag? That IS a bargain! I guess it IS insensitive to give the neighborhood kids kiwi fruit. I'll just pick up a few bags of Butterfingers."

And so it goes. A terrible cycle of gloom and doom. Take heed, my friend. Before it's all said and done, the average American spends approximately $79 on Halloween candy and an additional $200 on bigger jeans. And what about those darling little trick-or-treaters? They get stuck with Starlight mints left over from last year's Christmas party.

Thanksgiving Turkey and a Frozen Pizza

I'm cooking Thanksgiving dinner this year. The table will be set with the good china and a lovely cornucopia will be the centerpiece. My whole family will have a dandy old-fashioned time of peace and togetherness. At least that's what I'm telling them they will have. My parents, brother, sister-in-law, niece, and nephew are traveling to our Dresden home from Texas. I'm cooking turkey, dressing, the whole nine yards. I want to lend a hand of support and encouragement to those of you who, like me, will be preparing the traditional feast this year.

A few helpful hints to all novice Thanksgiving cooks:

1. Buy four frozen pepperoni pizzas to keep in the freezer. Put a sticky note on the pizzas that reads, "Back-up Plan." Don't ask questions. Just do it.

2. The frozen turkey package will say, "Thaw for 2-3 days in the refrigerator." Who are they kidding? If you didn't put that bird in the refrigerator in late September, forget it. (See hint #1)

3. Boiling a solidly frozen 15 lb. turkey in a big pot on the stove midnight before Thanksgiving Day will not work. (See hint #1)

4. Reach inside the raw turkey and remove that whole myriad of things you don't want to know the origin of. Take it all and throw it in the trash. Forget giblet gravy. Giblet gravy is like hotdogs and bologna. If people knew what they were eating, they'd come to their senses.

5. IF the meal turns out less than perfect, distract your guests by pulling out favorite board games like Scrabble. When Uncle Harold and Aunt Mildred start fighting over whether "redneck" is one word or two…the battle is all but won.

6. Don't be deceived into thinking you can substitute cake, cookies, or pudding for the traditional Thanksgiving pie. People want pie. Trust me. Pie. P-I-E. A "store bought" pie can easily be slid out of the disposable foil pie pan and into the lovely glass pie pan Aunt Constance gave you as a wedding present. (This is sheer speculation on my part.)

7. If you're scared of cooking the bird, buy a pre-cooked ham instead. This is impossible to mess up. Well, almost impossible. One time I bought a pre-cooked ham and it must have fallen out of the bag in the trunk of my car. A few days later, my boys said, "Something smells like blue cheese and wet dogs." This is when we learned what a 5-day old unrefrigerated ham smells like in the back of a Saturn. (I don't have to tell you that it's morally wrong to serve a ham which has been in the trunk of your car for five days, right? Just in case: IF your pre-cooked ham has been rolling around in the warmth of your trunk for 4 or 5 days, you MUST not serve it to your guests. No. Not even to Uncle Harold and Aunt Mildred. Dispose of it quickly before the temptation becomes too great.

8. Your relatives love you for who you are…even if the green bean casserole is too salty, the pies are all burnt, and the bird is too dry. (Who am I kidding? Get it right or you'll be the laughing stock of every family gathering from now on.)

9. Unplug the TV until everyone has eaten leisurely, shared their Thanksgiving blessings, kissed the cook, and played at least one round of Scrabble or Dominoes.

10. Remember to be thankful. We are more than blessed.

Meat Grinders and Digital Clocks

It's less than 50 days until Christmas. Yep! Less than 50 days to clamor through the endless sale ads, trudge through the store aisles, shop the internet, and wonder what to get relatives who already have everything they could possibly want or need.

I'm a horrible Christmas shopper. It's not that I don't love the people on my list. Oh, I love them alright. I probably would have been a good shopper in the late 1800's...when buying a kid an orange made him shout, "Oh, Mummy, you're the dandiest mummy ever!" I probably could have gotten into the concept of giving presents back when people sewed their own underwear and didn't know the meaning of "take-out pizza." But not now. We're all a bit spoiled and it takes some of the fun out of Christmas shopping.

If you were planning to get fresh fruit for the kids on your list this year, think again. A tangelo doesn't thrill a kid's heart like it used to. Oh, and don't bother giving kids underwear. My grandparents gave us underwear for Christmas during my growing up years. Every year, my cousins and I would open the ever-familiar soft sided package as if we had no clue. And then with resounding enthusiasm we'd yell, "Underwear! Just what I needed! Thanks, Granny and Pappa!" Yeah. That's back when kids were taught manners. Back when kids knew how to express the appropriate underwear appreciation. I'd be afraid to try it today.

I never know what to get people for Christmas. Some of you may be wondering what to get Grandma this year. I've absolutely no idea. She still hasn't opened that Chantilly dusting powder you gave her last year. I'm serious. Check her bathroom closet. It's still there, isn't it? Wrapped in the original cellophane with the red bow on top. And the pretty pink house shoes you gave her the year before? Check the hall closet. I'm serious. Go ahead and check. That's what I thought. Still in the original $19.99 box covered in holly berries. I know. Tragically disappointing. Oh, the fondue set you gave her in 1997? Don't even ask. I don't have the heart to tell you.

America's blatant prosperity has caused retailers to stoop to new lows as far as I'm concerned. They know Grandma hasn't opened the fondue set or the dusting powder, so they've tried to convince us to go in new directions. Meat grinders, talking clocks, electric back massagers. My word.

When opening a credit card bill recently, an advertisement popped out for a special digital clock which can tell time, inform you of the temperature, and pick up radar communication with a stealth bomber…or something like that. Anyway, I laughed and laughed as the bottom of the ad said, "Be the first one in your neighborhood to own one." I pictured my husband and me running up and down our country road yelling at the top of our lungs, "The clock! The clock! Nanny Nanny Boo Boo. WE'VE got the clock!" That's when the 3rd grade flashbacks hit my mind. Little Susie Carter standing near the water fountain wearing her new white go-go boots and bragging about the Mystery Date game she got for Christmas. OK. No time for therapy. Here's my simple minded holiday advice:

Don't obsess about Christmas shopping. Be moderate with children. (They'll thank you later.) Give to those in need. Enjoy a beautiful Tennessee autumn and eat a tangelo with a thankful heart.

The Big Tent and the Manger

I like my parents. Sure, I love them. But maybe more importantly, I like them. I respect the values they hold and the humility with which they hold them. Last week, my parents were on a work mission in Gulfport, Mississippi, helping victims of Katrina. Dad worked on houses. Mom cooked and served meals. Their group of 50 was led by John Lovelace. They worked with an organization called God's Katrina Kitchen, which serves meals to hundreds of people every day. The meals were for the volunteer workers and the homeless and the "everyone." My mom describes it so beautifully in the following words she wrote about the big tent:

"It looked like a circus tent with red and white stripes but inside there were Christmas lights, a Christmas tree, a nativity scene. There were people eating good food. Homeless people with their back packs containing a sleeping bag and all their possessions. Young families living in FEMA trailers a few yards away. Other locals in the area barely making it because of job loss related to Katrina. Long-time volunteers from many states and Canada. Members of a Recovery group. Trusty prison inmates working on houses. Short-term volunteers of every description: doctors, lawyers, merchants, and even old retirees like us. Reduced to one big pile of humanity because we all got hungry and we all came to the tent to eat scrambled eggs and grits or chicken and rice or whatever. When people go to work, really work, they don't wear their Sunday-go-to-meetin' clothes and they don't wear make-up and jewelry. So, in this red and white striped tent, we all looked the same."

The minute I read her description of the big tent, I thought back 2000 years ago to the manger in Bethlehem. Stinky animals. Dust and dung. Political turmoil. Civil unrest. Rich men living in prosperity. Uneducated shepherds tending to sheep. Wise men studying the stars. Prostitutes in the back alleys of Jerusalem. Carpenters building tables and chairs. Priests fulfilling their duties in the temple.

And they all were reduced to one big pile of humanity because they were hungry. They had a need. They all needed the same thing...a Savior. Forgiveness.

And in the midst of the dusty cave-like stable, a king was born. A king who would reign like no other. A king who would humbly wash people's feet. A king who would cuddle little children and confront political leaders. A king who would turn over the money changers' tables and forgive prostitutes. A king who would walk and live among us. A king who would die and rise again to purchase our redemption. A king who would gather us under the big tent and feed us and love us...even though He knew we were all prisoners. Even though He knew what all of us had done. We had robbed a convenience store or been proud of the fact we hadn't. We had drunk too much or gossiped about someone who did. We had been sexually immoral or we had been angry and critical. We had all loved too little and we all had the same need.
But then a king was born. What a glorious day! A king who could say with authority to all who would open their hearts, "I forgive you. I love you. You are clean. You are mine."

Today in Gulfport, Mississippi, a mass of humanity is gathering under the big tent for a good meal and a loving word about the Savior. Millions around the world are joining them. Just a tiny foretaste of the glorious gathering yet to come.

Holiday Help for Harried Women

I know. It's Christmas time. You're busy. You're saying, "Lisa, I don't have time to read the column. Must shop. Must bake. Must decorate. Must wrap. Must lose twenty pounds so I can wear the red velvet Christmas dress to the Christmas Eve party." Stop. Stop what you're doing. Put down that Christmas list, Girlfriend. Get your hand out of the chocolate chip bag, Sister. Listen up. It's time for tough love. If you're going to remain emotionally and physically healthy during this holiday season, you're going to have to listen carefully and stay calm. I'm going to lay down a few ground rules.

Rule #1: Stop watching Martha Stewart. I'm serious. If you continue watching the Martha Stewart show or reading the Martha Stewart magazine, you'll need a mood altering drug by the 15th. Martha is not a human being. Trust me. Human beings don't grind their own cloves or make handmade wreaths out of holly berries and orange peel.

Rule #2: Be creative with appetizers. Forget the time-consuming homemade cheese balls or hot artichoke dips for your Christmas party. Artichokes? Please. Only people who grind their own cloves eat artichokes. Be a renegade party planner. Take a 1 lb. package of beef bologna. Take a 12 oz. package of overly-pasteurized cheese slices. Cut into triangles and place on Ritz crackers. Ta-dah! You're a star.

Rule #3: Stop over-shopping for your precious little angels. Your kids have plenty of stuff. Let's do a little exercise, shall we? Walk into your child's room. Stand there for a moment. Now, as you observe your surroundings, do you find that there is a sad and depressing void of stimulation and activity? Precisely my point. Just remember, Abraham Lincoln walked several miles a day and read books by candle light. (No, I'm not sure what that has to do with Christmas. I just like to walk around reminding people of it.)

Rule #4: Aunt Betsy is not going to like the present you choose, regardless of the time you spend worrying about it. You know Aunt Betsy. You can't please her. Stop trying. Donate money to Samaritan's Purse or another help organization in her name. Then, give her a box of chocolate-covered cherries with a note about the donation and call it done. If she complains, send her my e-mail address. I can take her.

Rule #5: If you don't get all your Christmas cards sent, no one's life will be altered in any significant way. I'm serious. The world will continue spinning on its axis. I promise that your third cousin in Birmingham will not be pacing the floor day and night wondering why she hasn't received a picture of your family to stick on her refrigerator with a smiley face magnet. She still has the one from last year with little Billy's finger up his nose. Things haven't really changed that much, have they?

Rule #6: Married gals, don't forget romance during these next few weeks. If you tend to stay up late at night chopping fresh figs for Aunt Harriett's fruit cake or making homemade bows, you might consider a slightly more "creative" use of your time. If your gifts are adorned with cheap bows and you never get around to making fruit cake, it won't matter one little bit as long as you and your husband are playing footsy at the breakfast table. You can take that to the bank.

Well, that's it. My mission is complete. I'm holding up a cup of eggnog to toast your newfound holiday freedom! And in the words of that ever-popular modern day philosopher, "YOU GO, GIRL!"

Chapter 5

Testosterone is in the Air: Surviving an All-Male Household

A Man and His Chainsaw

I may have made a mistake. A big mistake. My beloved husband turned 40 this week. I knew I couldn't buy him a pair of khaki pants and a dress shirt in honor of this milestone birthday. No. To a 40-year-old man, a gift of khaki pants and a dress shirt would serve only to remind him that he's a person who goes to bed at 10:00, takes vitamins, and thinks about his retirement savings. No. For the 40th birthday, the gift needs to be big. It needs to be reckless and exciting. It needs to be nothing but sheer masculine testosterone-dripping power...nothing that can be ironed, controlled, or placed on a shelf.

A Harley-Davidson was my first thought. I could envision my bearded 40-year-old husband flying down University Drive on a Harley wearing a bandana, leather boots, black leather chaps, khaki pants, and a light blue oxford shirt. He'd be the picture of pure joy waving at the other professors as if to say, "Gosh, my wife loves me, doesn't she?" On second thought, maybe I should just have the words "mid-life crisis" tattooed on his forehead instead. Visions of the Harley soon faded as I realized it was too expensive anyway. I knew he'd love a pick-up truck. But again, too much cash. Time was ticking and the ideas were all too expensive.

Late one night the light bulb came on. We live on 16 acres of wooded paradise. My husband is a forester. He often speaks of limbs that need to be cut and trees that need to go. What says "I'm a man's man" more than a shiny brand-new 50cc of raw tree-slashing power? The decision was made. I finally had it. I knew this purchase had the potential to make me a widow within the year.....but, my dear husband was worth it.

When he unwrapped the massive gift, there was pure joy in his eyes. He was holding a box filled with power. No khaki pants here. He was now master of every tree's destiny within 16 acres. I began to get a little afraid. I knew he wanted to throw on his white t-shirt, old work boots, and Saturday overalls and take out some limbs. I feared that human limbs would be the first to go.

Don't get me wrong. My husband knows how to safely wield power tools. He was raised in the country. He doesn't have soft hands and he knows what a day's work feels like. If anyone could responsibly handle the chainsaw, he would be the one. But power is a strange and dangerous thing. A man gets a certain dazed look in his eyes when he hears the siren song of a roaring chainsaw. I wondered if our wooded paradise would look like a harvested Kansas wheat field within six months.

I noticed a strangely similar look in the eyes of both my boys, too. Suddenly I felt very alone. The boys could hardly wait to throw on their rubber boots and slash some wood. Forget getting their driver's licenses. Forget begging for a 4-wheeler. They would now focus all their attention on when they would be old enough to use the chainsaw. They wanted to hear the roar of the engine and wear the leather work gloves. They wanted to wipe their sweaty brows with a tattered bandana and yell, "Timber."

I'm happy to report that as of this writing, everyone in my family has all their extremities. The wooded acres are still wooded. My husband is a happy camper. And my little boys look forward to the day they'll wield the powerful chainsaw themselves. I have no problem with that. I merely request that they wait until I'm dead.

Why do Men Love Flashlights?

I've yet to meet a man who doesn't love flashlights. It's the illuminating power, the triumphing over darkness, the power to see where mortal man has never seen. No man ever goes into a hardware store talking about a paisley tie he got for Christmas. Men want power to light up the night. Paisley ties don't represent that kind of power.

In our house, the various flashlights and their batteries are revered. If one of the boys leaves a flashlight on, it's a family felony. My husband is fond of saying, "If these flashlight batteries run down, we won't have light in a power shortage or other disaster." Yeah. It would be a tragedy not to huddle around the radio shining light on each other's faces at a point of utter doom. And of course, we'd hate to resort to a candle or the coal oil lamp. No one could ever survive with just those. Poor Abe Lincoln. How did he even become president? There were no flashlights.

My husband is a wonderful man. I'm serious. No man was ever more God honoring, family focused, financially conservative, and just an all around good guy. I've been married to him for 16 years. But moving to the country recently has brought out a whole Marshall Dillon side of his personality.

Last week he came home with a flashlight the size of Colorado. The conversation went something like this,
"Honey, I'm home!"

"Sweetie, what is that monstrous looking thing you're carrying?"

"It's a flashlight. It's a spotlight. With this thing, we can REALLY see into the woods at night."

"Sweetie, why do we want to stand on our back porch and see into the woods at night?"

"Oh, lots of reasons. We might see wildlife. Or what if we hear a noise? We'll be able to fully investigate it now."

If we hear a noise, I prefer to get in the bed, pull up the covers, and pretend I don't hear anything. If the noise persists, I'm for calling 911. I don't have the slightest inkling to "investigate" anything.

That night after the kids were in bed, we decided to take that puppy out for a spin. We stood out on the back porch and pointed the massive beacon of light toward the woods. I thought the sheer glow was going to wake the children and uproot the plants.

"Look, Lisa, did you see that squirrel?"

"Honey, a family of four in Idaho thinks you're sending a distress signal. People in Union City think there's a car sale going on here. Yes, Sweetie, I saw the squirrel."

Men. I'll never fully understand them. It starts when they're boys. Boys can't leave a stick on the ground. I have two boys. They've never once passed a stick they didn't pick up. They can smell a stick from at least two miles. One day one of my boys picked up a stick and said, "Don't worry, Mom. If bad guys come into our yard, I'll protect you." I don't know if bad guys would be afraid of a 40 lb. boy wearing cowboy boots, shorts, and a tank top. But I appreciate the sentiment.

I love men and boys. I love the fact that they want to conquer darkness and protect us against evil. I love my flashlight-wielding husband too. I really can't complain. He didn't say a word when I wanted to shop for new bathroom rugs because the ones from the old house didn't match the bathrooms in the new house. I'm sure replacing perfectly good rugs made no sense to him. But he pushed the cart happily through the housewares section with a smile on his face. He was probably daydreaming about lighthouse signals he'd send from the backyard.

Soggy Camping Reveals Character

Camping is one of those things that sounds like a great idea...about a month before the actual trip. It starts when you're sitting around the dining room table with your lovely family. Somebody says, "Hey! Let's go camping during Spring Break!" Everyone at the table says in unison, "Yeah! Let's do it!" Our family has been on many camping trips together. But it's as if we've forgotten what camping actually means. When we're sitting in a warm house eating meatloaf and mashed potatoes with silverware, the memory of real tent camping is somehow removed from our psyche. We cheer and get all enthusiastic at the prospects of a camping trip as though we don't have the slightest idea of the misery it will entail.

Our family went camping during Spring Break. Our kids better remember it and remember it well. I mean, they better tell camping stories for the rest of their natural lives. If one of them becomes the Valedictorian, the FIRST thing that better come out of his mouth during the graduation speech is, "My parents are the greatest...they took us camping." That's the primary reason parents go camping. It's all about the memories.

Our camping trip began with a challenge. Four people, lots of camping gear, one small Saturn. My ingenious husband managed to get coolers, tents, food, clothes, and of course, flashlights, into a space smaller than a sock drawer. People should get college credit for just watching the process. We piled all the stuff on the driveway and it looked like an impossibility. He walked around the massive pile like an Olympic athlete making mental notes. Then, he cracked his knuckles and did the impossible. He got it all in. Of course, the last few items had to be added after the kids and I were in the car. We each were given a snorkel so we could breathe.

The campsite in Middle Tennessee was lovely. We were near the water and the trees were ablaze with fall color. It was cold but we brought lots of flannel and all seemed right with the world. The greatest camping joy for my two boys was helping Dad build a fire. If there's one thing I've learned in an all-male family it's that men have a natural affinity with fire. What is it about fire that intrigues 6, 8, and 40 year old boys so much? Fire represents power. My boys set sticks on fire and made torches. They then marched around the site ready to battle any enemy. I didn't bother telling them that there were no evil enemies at a Corps of Engineers camp site in Middle Tennessee.

As darkness fell, it grew colder. We huddled. We cuddled. We tried to remain optimistic. Then, it happened. Hard, cold, unforgiving sheets of rain fell from the sky. Cold is one thing. Cold and wet is quite another. We took refuge in the nearby bathhouse. Eventually we ran back to the tent and decided to call it a night. We piled the blankets on top of the sleeping bags and attempted sleep.

If you want to see someone's character, place him on an air mattress that's losing air in a small tent with rain pelting down and temperatures dropping. After we had all gotten snuggled in, our littlest camper said with sobs, "I'm weally thirsty. I'm getting dehydwated." I have never loved my husband of sixteen years more than I loved him at that moment. Without saying a word, he rose from the warmth of the sleeping bag and put on soggy clothes. He walked to the car to retrieve the needed drinks. He didn't want anyone to get "dehydwated." What a man! At that moment, I resolved something in my mind. If my kids become famous someday and the camera turns toward them, they'll probably say, "Hi Dad!" I can live with that.

Men and the New Colors

I'm not hip. I know I'm not hip. Every day I see how society is moving forward in all things trendy without my input or understanding. Hence, my latest revelation. I don't know the colors. I'm serious. I am an uneducated person in regard to the names of colors. I thought that begging my mom for the 64 pack of Crayola crayons in second grade would make me color savvy. But evidently it didn't.

A catalog arrived in the mail this week. This particular catalog was advertising clothes for men. God bless the men of America. Here are just a few of the colors listed for men's shirts (and no, I'm not making this up): apricot frost, bonny blue, peacock, banana, parchment, celadon, and flame. I know. It doesn't make sense to me either.

No man wants to say to the retail phone operator, "I'll take 3 extra-large polo shirts…oh, the colors? Well, um, yeah, uh, well, just whatever you think is best."

"Sir, I'll need your color choices."

"Well, um, let me move to the phone in the back room. OK, that's 3 extra-large polo shirts in bonny blue, banana, and flame."

Poor guy. No man should be asked to say "bonny blue, banana, and flame" all in the same sentence. How can a man maintain his masculine dignity under those circumstances?

The pants colors are equally confusing. Here are a few options: cement, eucalyptus, French vanilla, bark, moonlight, balsam, and bean. I'm guessing the colors were invented by a group of 30-something latte-drinking women living on the coast of California. Can you imagine a big ol' country boy calling a retail operator and saying, "I'll take two pairs of 40X34 pants. One in french vanilla and the other in moonlight. And throw in an extra-large apricot frost shirt to go with the eucalyptus pants I bought last month." And people wonder why men don't act like men anymore.

Men need to stand up and revolt against this ridiculous trend. I'm calling all men to change their ordering habits. Don't fall prey to their crafty little plan. If you start ordering bonny blue shirts and balsam pants, what will be next? Next, they'll want you to order briefcases in colors that match your shoes. They'll expect you to wear socks that match your shirt. Men of America, this is a call to action. Don't slide down this slippery slope or you'll soon be wearing girdles and tweezing your eyebrows.

When you call in a clothing order simply say, "I'd like 3 extra-large polo shirts in blue, yellow, and red."

 The operator will then say, "Sir, I'm afraid those color choices are not listed in my computer."

Your response is simply, "I will be glad to repeat my order. I'd like 3 extra-large polo shirts in blue, yellow, and red."

The operator's response, "I can only sell the shirt colors which are listed in my computer. Are you referring to bonny blue, banana, and flame?"

Don't get mad. Stay calm and simply say, "Ma'am, when I see a woman changing a tire on the side of the road, I stop and change the tire for her. I open doors for women. I still eat red meat. I don't want to wear a girdle or tweeze my eyebrows. I just want a red shirt." I know. You feel better already.

We Taught Our Boys about Organizing

On a cool and dreary Saturday morning, a decision was made. The boys were watching cartoons. My husband and I were drinking coffee with our feet propped up on the footstools. All seemed perfectly beautiful and serene on a little country road outside Dresden. But in the midst of the serenity and caffeine-induced utopia, trouble was brewing.

An idea was born. The idea was conceived in my brain and unfortunately came charging out my mouth like a runaway freight train. No one could see it coming. No one had time to step on the brakes. A crash of epic proportions was inevitable.

"Hey, Guys, I have a GREAT idea. Considering the fact that we can barely walk through your room or the play room, let's move every single thing out of both rooms into the hallway. We'll pile it to the ceiling if we have to. When it's all out, we'll sort and organize the stuff and put it back neatly in your room and the play room. What happiness it will be for all!"

Dead silence. Jelly-smeared faces looked pale and skeptical. But we were ready. We sold the Saturday morning organizing event like a prize fight at Madison Square Gardens.

"Boys, think how GREAT this will be! Nothing's more fun than piling junk up in the hallway! Why, I can hardly wait to get started! I wonder how high we can pile the stuff. Let's hurry! We don't want to miss a minute of the fun!"

Still jelly-smeared and skeptical, our two little charges joined in the "fun" and we proceeded to empty two entire rooms into the hallway. It was 8:30 on a Saturday morning and I was on top of the world. I felt good. No. Better than good. I felt great! My husband and I were teaching our boys about organization and tidiness. All four of us were working on a project together. The train was running down the tracks and not a derailment in sight. Who could have known the hazards that lay ahead?

Piling stuff was a lot of fun. Piling. Piling. Piling. Fun. Fun. Fun. But all good things must come to an end. At about 10:00, we realized everything had been piled in the hallway. The caffeine was wearing off. Enthusiasm was slowly dying. Flying a kite seemed like an appropriate diversion. But, no.

"Okay now. Well, we've got all this junk, I mean stuff, piled up out here. Yes sirree. It's all piled up. Yep, right here in the hallway. Why, just look at it all. Mismatched dirty socks. Pajamas we haven't seen since last spring. Gigantic toys designed to overtake the modern American home. It's a virtual tower of super heroes, Halloween costumes, and broken crayons. And look, here's the craft project you guys made in Bible School last year. Yep, sure is. Who would have ever thought that all this stuff has been living in just two little rooms? Yeah, who'd have ever thought?"

Again, dead silence.

Eventually, the silence was broken.

"Uh, Mom, what are we supposed to do now? I mean, how are we supposed to put all this stuff back?"

Shoot. That's where the whole idea became foggy. The train was embarking on a dangerous curve and I was craving a bologna sandwich.

"Well, I say we put half of it in garbage bags and see if it wouldn't be happier living in the big garbage cans on the carport."

Both boys stared at me as though I were speaking Russian. But, it was worth it. We eventually removed every item from the hallway. We taught our boys about the joy of organizing. Feel free to come see their beautiful rooms. Just don't look in the closets or under the beds.

How Does a Boy Become a Man?

Raising kids is entertaining and enlightening. A few days ago one of my boys was in a very contemplative mood and said quite seriously, "Mom, do you know what I'm going to do when I grow up?"

"Are you going to discover a cure for cancer?" "No."
"Become an astronaut and live on the space station?" "No."
"Are you going to be a missionary in a foreign land?" " No."

"Mom, when I grow up I'm going to buy a TV with a screen as big as our house and I'm going to watch TV all day and all night."

I had to laugh. My son is a boy. He thinks like a boy. Because his TV time is currently limited, he thinks he'd like to have the ultimate media freedom. His dreams are not man-size yet. That's okay.

Not long ago, my other son said, "Mom, when my brother and I grow up, we're going to live in a cave with a mountain lion and a panther for pets. We'll also have 100 regular cats and a few dogs, too."

My reply was calm and simple, "What about getting married?"

"Oh Mom, we CAN'T get married. Getting married would be impossible!"

"Why would it be impossible?"

"Mom, we can't get married. Don't you know that girls don't like to live in caves with mountain lions and panthers???"

"Silly me. What was I thinking? Why yes, most women would hardly want to live in a cave with you and your brother and a mountain lion and a panther. And let me say that if you DO meet a woman who wants to live in a cave with you, your brother, a mountain lion, a panther, 100 cats, a few dogs, and a mega screen TV.....I think you should snatch her up in a New York minute. I think you'll know you've met 'the one,' don't you?"

We enjoy raising little boys. They bring such joy to our adult lives. But our hope is that sometime in the next 10-15 years, they'll grow into men. I don't know exactly how that process is going to unfold. How does a boy grow into a man? And why do so many boys reach chronological adult age.....but are still far from manhood?

I'm concerned. I spend enough time with college students to see that some young men in their 20's have reached manhood while sadly others seem trapped in the throes of a second boyhood. I can't explain all the reasons why some boys transition into manhood and others retain their boyhood, sometimes even into their 30's and 40's. But we're committed even now to helping them make the transition.

One of the greatest joys of my life would be looking at both of them as adults and knowing that somehow, despite parental inadequacies, God developed them into mature and selfless men. What qualities do I believe a real man possesses? Here are just a few:

A real man goes to the store in the middle of the night in a thunderstorm for kids' Tylenol. He pulls his car over when he sees a woman changing a tire. He makes money but doesn't seem troubled that it all goes to the needs of the family. In fact, he seems happy about providing for others, even when it means there's nothing left for his own wants. People from all walks of life feel equally comfortable in his presence. He doesn't talk about himself all the time. He is physically affectionate with his wife and verbally appreciative of everything she does. He plays Frisbee, even when he's tired. He reads books and never stops learning. He's humble and recognizes his need for God. He prays with little children. And he prays alone. He doesn't dream about video games and vehicles because he's busy dreaming about becoming a better leader. Real men lead by serving others.

That's what I want for my boys. I want them each to have the privilege of becoming a man like their dad. And if they can become that man and still live in a cave, I'll be cheering them on.

Chapter 6

Home is Where the Heart Is: But Don't Open the Hall Closet

Messies vs. Cleanies

Here's my dilemma. When I live messy, I can't find anything. When I live clean, I've thrown everything I need away. When I live messy, I dig through piles of junk mail trying to find the babysitter's phone number. When I live clean, I realize her phone number was with a pile of junk mail that I threw in the trash yesterday. Either way, no phone number. I'm a person who is destined to never have the babysitter's phone number. I understand this. I embrace this.

Messy people hide things. It's what we do. Oh, we can have company quite frequently. The house looks stellar upon company's arrival. What our company doesn't know is what happened with a 30-gallon garbage bag an hour before they arrived. Messy people, take heart. I know you're getting nervous thinking I'm going to reveal one of our trade secrets. Take a deep breath and remember that confession is good for the soul. Messy people "bag" things. There. I said it. We need a 12-step program for out-of-control "bagging." Right before company comes, we get a clean 30-gallon garbage bag and we zoom through the house like the Tasmanian Devil on a mission to throw suntan lotion, junk mail, old magazines, flip flops, dirty dishes, clean clothes, unpaid bills, school permission slips, and overdue library books in a garbage bag. There have been times I've mistakenly "bagged" one of my children because they were sitting so still in front of the TV. The bag is then deposited in an undisclosed location to be dealt with at a later time.

Clean people are still in shock after reading the "bagging" confession. I know. Clean people are saying to each other over coffee, "Gertrude, did she say she 'bags' things? What in the world does she mean? Why is she 'bagging' things? Why are there things that need to be 'bagged'?"

Must I spell it out for you? Must I weep and pour out my very SOUL? Okay, Cleanies. I'm only going to explain this one time. Stuff is lying around our house in places it doesn't belong. Yes, in places it doesn't belong. Many of the items in our house have never even found a home. They're indigent items. That's how they end up in the bag of shame.

Clean people don't "bag" things. But they need not feel haughty or self-righteous. Oh no. Clean people could use a 12-step program of their own. Cleanies have their own little rituals before company comes. They pick microscopic pieces of fuzz off the carpet. They sweep under rugs and use strange vacuum attachments. They even clean their oven. May I let you in on a little secret? Unless an animal has crawled into your oven and died a painful death, an oven doesn't need to be cleaned. It's an oven. It's a place where you bake things. It's not a tea room where you entertain guests. Cleanies, I'm saying this because I love you. On your death bed you may end up regretting the hours you spent cleaning the oven with that toxic substance. Think about why your messy friends live longer. Less exposure to cleaning fumes.

I'd love to keep writing about this ever-important subject. But company is on the way and my boys can't find their shoes. Why can't they remember to look in the garbage bag in the guest bathtub?

Brad Pitt vs. Pappa

I don't get it. I still hear women on talk shows or radio programs swooning for Brad Pitt. For those of you who don't keep up with Hollywood current affairs, let me take a moment to enlighten you. Brad Pitt is a multi-millionaire movie star with a very distinct track record when it comes to women. He falls "madly in love" and then tends to fall "madly out of love" a few years later. His most public split was with recent wife, Jennifer Anniston, after he fell for Angelina Jolie while working with her on a movie.

If you're a woman who swoons for Brad Pitt, may I have a word with you? Take a breath. Take a good look at Brad's track record and ask yourself these pivotal questions:

1. Would Brad Pitt enjoy sharing a funnel cake at the Soybean Festival?
2. Does he know how to laugh and chop wood at the same time?
3. Would he get up with a sick kid in the middle of the night?
4. Does he yell, "I'm a lucky man!" when he smells pinto beans and cornbread?
5. Does he know the definition of the word "faithful?"

I know. Brad Pitt comes up terribly short when you really analyze the facts. Women, let's contrast Brad Pitt and his obvious shortcomings with the life of my Pappa Pryor. When you compare and contrast...well, you can come up with your own conclusions.

My pappa spent most of his life as a teacher and a principal. Granny ironed his white shirts every day for more than 40 years as he educated multiple generations of West Kentuckians. Sometime after 4 p.m. each day, he came home, changed into overalls, and thus transformed himself into a farmer. He and Granny often spent time working side by side in the garden or tending to the cattle. They didn't hug and kiss in public. But as my mom would later write, "I never doubted their love for each other."

Pappa and Granny raised four kids who all married and raised 13 kids who all married and are in the process of raising 26 kids. Pappa and Granny worshipped and served at the same country church all their lives. He was a tender leader who often wept during prayer. Always impressed with Granny's Biblical scholarship, he depended on her in many ways. They respected each other's intellect and incredible work ethic. I believed they could do anything...together.

Pappa was the epitome of a soft-spoken, scholarly, southern gentleman. He had found what some people search for their whole lives. Contentment. His calling as an educator and his love for farming produced a fulfilling life outside a small Kentucky town. He and his bride lived in the same house for more than 50 years. And it still smells like fried apples.

I never once saw anyone ask Pappa for his autograph. Not even once. Pappa died and Granny's Alzheimer's disease has robbed her of the memories. But the legacy continues. Pappa was a real man. A man who never stood Granny up for supper because he had to catch a plane. A man who found peace and satisfaction in one little corner of this big world. A man who could love one woman for more than a half century. Brad Pitt and his new girlfriend, Angelina, are on the cover of almost every magazine on the face of the earth right now. They're busy jet setting all around the world. But, I feel terribly sorry for Angelina. I doubt she'll ever be as blessed as Granny was. Angelina is experiencing the "temporary affection" of a famous man. Granny knew the real love of a good man. She was the blessed one.

Time for Spring Cleaning

It's time to "come clean." I know. Some of you are hyper-clean and organized year round, 24 hours a day, 7 days a week. If you wipe down your baseboards with Murphy's Oil Soap and a chamois cloth every Sat. morning at 8:00, step away from this column. Go away and come back next week.

For the rest of you, take my hand. I'm here for you. Do you have a hall closet that you can't open because you'll be hit in the head with a 1978 softball trophy, a faded box of "Twister," and a reindeer Christmas wreath? Does your laundry room serve as a storage place for broken toys and old prom dresses? Did your grandma tell you it was a sin to throw away old jelly jars? Oh sweet friend, I've been there. I'm here to encourage you. You probably need to see a therapist. But, for some of you, a lowly newspaper columnist will have to do. Take a deep cleansing breath. In, out. In, out. In, out. Repeat after me, "I can be free of annoying clutter. Freedom. Sweet freedom."

It's time to roll up your sleeves, play some upbeat music, put on the gas mask...and do some spring cleaning. But before we can begin cleaning, we must take some time to "de-clutter." And before we can de-clutter, we must adjust our minds. Let's start telling the truth, shall we? Frequently people say, "We're just outgrowing our house. Our house is just too small." Let's clarify that. You're not outgrowing your house...your STUFF is outgrowing your house. You and the human beings you love can easily squeeze into the space currently provided. It's the STUFF that might have to take a hike. There. There. Some of you are getting a bit tearful. You're saying that I've no idea how valuable your "stuff" is. What's that? Yes, I know. The plaid couch was given to you by Uncle Charlie before he passed on in '84. The laundry basket full of plastic bread bags may "come in handy" someday. You can never have too many jelly jars. The two tons of old magazines and newspapers currently rotting in the garage are great for kid's papier-mâché projects. The piles of old and faded bed sheets would be perfect for making costumes for a school play that involved the Roman Empire. Excuses. Excuses. May I address the above excuses? I promise to be sensitive and loving.

Uncle Charlie is gone…and he wants the plaid couch put out of its misery. No human being, even if he lives to be 110, will EVER be able to use 967 plastic bread bags. I promise. I know what your grandma said about jelly jars. Read my lips, "She made jelly." Do you make jelly? If you don't make jelly, free the jars. Your child would have to make a papier-mâché clown head AND a donkey piñata every 47 minutes for the rest of his natural life…in order to use 1/3 of the paper you have piled in the garage. No school in West Tennessee is getting ready to put on a play about the Roman Empire. IF, by chance, a school in West Tennessee DOES plan to put on a play about the Roman Empire, they won't know to call you to claim the old and faded bed sheets which are piled up under the coffee table. Trust me. The sheets want to be put out of their misery. Set them free, I tell you. Set them free.

I have faith in you. Yes, I know. Your head is spinning and you're feeling nauseous. Maybe you need a coffee break before hitting the clutter. Feel free to grab some chocolate. The carbohydrates will give you energy. Go through each room of your house and take ½ the stuff and put it in the garage. Give it away or have a garage sale. Don't tarry. Don't give yourself time to "re-think" the decision. Keep repeating the words, "Freedom. Sweet freedom." Tune in next week when I address one of the most interesting cultural activities of our era…the garbage sale…I mean, garage sale.

Garage Sale Therapy

Garage Sale. Two of the scariest words in the English language. People who host garage sales should post the following disclaimer sign in their yard: "I have junk piled up around my house that I don't want anymore. I want you to take this junk and pile it up around your house instead. For this privilege, I'm going to charge you money. However, because I can completely fill the trunk of your car for a mere $6, you'll hug me and thank me as though I've done you a favor. Truth is, in a few years, you'll turn around and sell these same items at your own garage sale for $3."

I had a garage sale once. In order to save some of you the trauma, I'll provide this written re-enactment.

It was a beautiful Texas spring when some friends and I decided to host "The Garage Sale of the Century." Heed my warning. Going in with seven friends makes garage sale hosting a logistical nightmare. At midnight before the sale, we were still labeling kids' clothes, ceramic duck candle holders, and college textbooks. I know. No one wants to buy old college textbooks. I'm fully aware of that now. The average garage sale shopper doesn't want a 10 lb. 1983 edition of "College Algebra." The half-used eye shadow and the rusty Fry Daddy were the bargains of choice. At 1:00 a.m., we were still stacking junk on tables. That's when a realization hit me right between the eyes. I was an idiot. My friends were idiots. We had spent $30 on pizza, $20 on labels, $35 on promotion, and had pooled several hundred "woman hours" in order to create the "Garage Sale of the Century." Between the Algebra textbook and the ceramic duck candle holder…I might clear enough to buy a cup of coffee. (And I don't mean Starbucks.)

The morning of the garage sale I received my education. I had no idea there were "professional garage sale participants." These people arrive at the sale in the middle of the night with special money belts, caffeine-induced cheerfulness, and a silver tongue. I was completely unprepared.

"What will you take on this ceramic duck candle holder with the fluorescent green label marked 50 cents?"

"Uh, I don't know. It's 5:00 a.m. and I've only slept 2 hours. How about 50 cents?" She could smell my naivety. It hung in the air and she was moving in for the kill.

"50 cents for THAT? Those are usually only 25 cents at garage sales."

That's when it happened. I had lost too much sleep, eaten too much pizza, consumed a year's worth of coffee in a 24-hour period...and I was breaking under the pressure. Tearfully, I handed the ceramic duck candle holder to the woman in question and said, "Here. Take it. It's free. Any woman who wants to get up in the middle of the night, strap on a money belt, and humiliate a sleep-deprived novice garage sale host...must need a ceramic duck candle holder pretty badly. Trust me. You deserve it. I'll even throw in a College Algebra book."

A dear friend recently hosted her first garage sale. She was amazed at the things people said and did. Let's be honest. For some people, garage sale shopping is like drinking alcohol. It removes much-needed inhibition. The minute you put a "garage sale" sign in your yard, people believe they can walk into your house, ride your bicycle, and make an offer on anything that isn't nailed down. She could have sold her car, her mailbox, and her elementary-aged child. Another warning. Be sure to set boundaries. Never let someone dig your mailbox out of the ground in front of your house. That's just plain wrong.

I know. Some of you have had perfectly successful garage sales. I respect you. I just can't do it. I thoroughly enjoy people but my ineptitude in marketing, money management, and organization just makes garage sale hosting too challenging for my feeble psyche. That's okay. I'm perfectly happy giving my stuff away. By the way, if you're looking for a 1984 Political Science textbook, give me a call.

Top 10 Reasons NOT to Spring Clean

Warning! Warning! It's March. Magazines and books are trying to convince you to invest your time spring cleaning. But don't fall prey to their wicked schemes. Come join the rally! Help me spread the word about all the great reasons NOT to do any spring cleaning this year. Here are my Top Ten Reasons NOT to Spring Clean:

#10. Do you really want to know what's in the guest room closet? (I didn't think so.)

#9. Spider webs offer opportunities for your children to learn the wonders of science, insect behavior, and the circle of life. (Would you DENY your children a valuable education just so the neighbors won't talk? Shame on you.)

#8. It's a waste of time to clean out behind the refrigerator. (If you get a sudden urge to pull out the refrigerator and see what's back there, stop! Stop, I tell you! I can tell you EXACTLY what's back there and it will save you the investigation. 2 dusty Christmas pictures, 4 crayons, a dried up piece of bologna, the birthday card you forgot to send your sister-in-law, two blue hamburger buns, and the October '03 telephone bill. You're welcome.)

#7. Dusty rugs and furniture cause your allergies to act up and when your allergies act up, you visit a local physician, which helps the local medical community make a living. (Spring cleaning is bad for local business.)

#6. No one looks at baseboards. (People who visit your house and DO look at baseboards should be escorted to the nearest therapist who will help them find a life.)

#5. There's no reason to clean out behind the washer/dryer when you know exactly what's back there. (Behind every washer/dryer are the following: 1 quarter, 3 nickels, 7 pennies, 1 white sock, a few unmentionables, 2 wrinkled baseball cards, and enough lint to make an overstuffed couch. Leave it alone. Just walk away.)

#4. Washing windows is morally wrong. (It just is. Trust me on this one.)

#3. If you're planning on cleaning underneath the beds, you might as well just rent a horror movie and seat your small kids in front of the TV. (Think about it. Do you want your kids to dream about 6 foot dust bunnies suffocating them while they sleep peacefully wrapped in their Spiderman comforter? Of course not. You're a bigger person than that.)

#2. The garage. Who said you have to be able to park your car in the garage? (Where's the "Homeowner's RULE book" which says every garage must contain a car? The magazines, Christmas wreaths, rusty tools, and craft projects "gone wrong" are all perfectly content filling up space in the garage. If you remove some of them or rearrange them…it will upset the delicate balance of nature. You're not an anti-environmentalist, are you?)

#1. Some people believe spring is the time to wash curtains and clean out the kitchen cabinets. (No. A thousand times no. Washing curtains wastes valuable water resources. Opening the kitchen cabinets will create a massive avalanche of empty Cool Whip containers, old hot cocoa packets, and plastic Wal-Mart bags. Turn back, Brave Warrior. Turn back.)

It's time for the Anti-Spring Cleaning movement to sweep the country. Help me spread the word! And if you find yourself experiencing a sudden urge to wash windows, turn on the Andy Griffith marathon instead. That's a clean experience the whole family can enjoy!

Put Down that Paintbrush!

Warning! When it comes to painting, hire a professional. Sell the car if you must. Take a second mortgage. Trust me on this one. The painful story which follows is a true and accurate portrayal. This written re-enactment has not been dramatized in any way. Please caution young readers.

It was an average day in early December. I decided it was time to paint the living room, guest room, and hallway. Mistake #1: Never decide to do a home improvement project in early December. If a middle-aged woman enters a paint store in early December, the store personnel should have the decency to ask her if she's gotten her Christmas cards sent, her shopping done, her tree up, and if she's made the annual batch of fudge for Uncle George. If the woman in question has not even started any of those projects, she should be politely refused the paint purchase until mid-January. No such luck for me.

I naively came home with three gallons of paint. I planned to paint the living room and hallway a tan color called "Crisp Khaki." Mistake #2: The color. Never paint your living room the color of an insurance salesman's pants. If you're going to paint, at least paint with a dramatic shade that people will notice. If you paint your living room the color of an insurance salesman's pants, no one even notices you've painted. Not one person entering our home has commented about our freshly painted walls. However, several people have said they felt an unusual desire to buy more life insurance.

It all began when I donned my Hawaiian knit Capri pants, faded red t-shirt, and my bright pink shower cap. I was a clown on a mission. Two friends had done a masterful job of helping me paint the dining room a few weeks back. They would have been more than willing to help with the living room. But I felt it was a little indecent to ask a friend to help with a painting project in early December. Besides, I was feeling confident that I could do the project solo. Mistake #3: Going solo. Never go solo. Painting is like swimming. It's dangerous without a buddy.

After about seven hours of painting, I realized I really liked the original color. I wanted to go back to my life before drop cloths and pink shower caps and "Crisp Khaki" under my fingernails...but no can do, my friends. Once you start slathering that thick stuff on the walls...you've made a commitment. No turning back. At one point, while coming down from a folding chair, I stuck my size ten foot in the paint tray and turned it over spilling the whole tray of paint. I know. You think I made that up for the paper. Yeah. Keep thinking that.

Here's the moral to the story. Choose to be happy with the color your walls are painted right now. Decide that they are lovely colors and make no plans to change them. You must make a pledge to yourself that crayon marks add character and purple bathrooms are fabulous. I'm serious. Every time you pass that chartreuse laundry room, just say to yourself, "I love chartreuse." Trust me! Do WHATEVER it takes to save yourself.

I never even got to our guest room. After the living room and the hallway were completed, I retired the shower cap and my aching muscles and decided I LOVED the guest room just the way it is.

There's something I'd like to share with my two sons in closing. Boys, someday when Daddy and I are dead and you're ready to sell the house, the realtor might suggest you paint the guest room. Look down in the shed on the white metal shelf. There will be an unopened can of lovely green paint. Knock yourself out. But don't say I didn't warn you.

How Clean is Your Car?

I'm not a psychologist, but I play one in the newspaper. I'm fascinated by human behavior. I fully believe I could write a Master's thesis about Mary Jane Doe's life if I had access to ONE thing only…her car. You can tell a LOT about a person by riding in her car.

The psychological study begins when you surprise Mary Jane by telling her you'll need to ride with her in her car. If she's a "clean car" person she never even breaks stride. She says things like, "Hop in." A "messy car" person stands amazed when the "clean car" person says, "Hop in." We're thinking, "Gosh, don't you have to haul all the junk out of my seat and sling it into the trunk with the ice chest from the 4th of July picnic and the old baby clothes you've been hauling around since last March to give to your friend, Marge." Think again. Neat and clean people don't have to do any of those things. They unloaded the ice chest on July 5th. They took the clothes to Marge the day they put them in the trunk. They're neat and tidy, remember? They do, however, say stupid things when you get in the car like, "Oh, pardon the mess. There's a gum wrapper in the back corner of the trunk. Let me grab that." The car's floor looks like it's just been vacuumed and then combed out with a hair brush. You don't smell cheap apple blossom air freshener. No. "Clean car" people almost always have air freshener that's called "new car smell." OR maybe, just maybe, they've actually kept the car so unbelievably clean that it still smells new even though it's three years old. Either way, it's a mystery to me.

Surprise a "messy car" person with the news that you'll be riding in the car with her. She'll get that blue-light-in-the-rearview-mirror look. She'll begin to sweat profusely and say things like, "Sure. That'll be great. Throw me two 30-gallon trash bags, a Dustbuster, a pine tree air freshener, and give me about 25 minutes." "Clean car" people have absolutely no understanding of this departure delay. It would be an education for the average neat and clean person to watch a messy person clean out the car. Sheer astonishment. Food bags, coke cans, books, junk mail, fingernail polish, garden tools, overdue library books, baked beans (don't ask.). And this is by no means an exhaustive list.

"Messy car" people are thrilled when they finally have kids. Whew! Now when people get in our car, we can say, "Pardon the mess. Egads! Those crazy kids…candy bar wrappers, coke cans, smelly gym clothes." Who are we kidding? The car looked just like that five years before we even had a kid. Kids, however, are a challenge for the owner of a clean car. The children of clean people must be rigorously taught the value of not piling happy-meal toys in the wheel well. They're taught never to get in the car within 30 minutes of eating peanut butter. It becomes an absolute…like waiting 30 minutes after a meal to go swimming.

Here's what I don't get. Even though I've struggled with messiness most of my adult life, I experienced a real break-through a few years ago in regard to our house. I learned the value of keeping it put together. You can come visit us most days even without warning. Now here's where the psychological study would be valuable. The house got better. The car got worse. It's almost as though too much success in tidiness would be dangerous to my health or humility. So, feel free to come see us anytime you want. But if you need a ride somewhere, call and make an appointment.

Chapter 7

Crazy Pets or Crazy People?

They Call it Puppy Love

I'm not a dog person. I'm not really a cat person either. I can barely tolerate the fish tanks at Red Lobster. I've just never been an animal lover. I realize this puts me in a less than humane light with some of you. But, find it in your heart to forgive me. I like people just fine. It's animals I seem to have issue with.

But, a few days ago something happened. A friend (and I use that term loosely) gave my family two puppies. According to my "friend," these two homeless puppies had been found on the side of the road shivering and miserable. Yeah. I'd like to see a police report supporting that story. She had the whole speech planned out, "Of course, if you don't want them, I can take them to the pound." Pause. Sigh. Guilt floating through the air. "They're both boys. Isn't that sweet? You've got two boys and here are two little boy puppies." Yeah. Grab a tissue. I'm speechless.

I know some of you have considered us less than good parents because our boys have never had a pet. Personally, I think I have an excellent defense. I didn't want a pet and preschoolers at the same time. I didn't think changing diapers and scooping up after a dog were activities that should occur simultaneously. But now my boys are in school. They're growing up. They throw fewer tantrums and rarely get up in the night. And of course, they want a dog. We thought having great parents would be enough for them. But, no.

I kept looking in the box at those two little puppies. All I could think of was the mess and the trouble. What if they whimper at night? In the end though, I thought of my kids. They would be overjoyed. I took the mongrel puppies out of sheer love for my boys, ages 6 and 8. I felt like "Mom of the

Year." Now my boys would have a chunk of the "American Dream."

I came home and proudly deposited the two boy brothers with the two dog brothers in the backyard. When they saw the puppies, it was as though a flashlight had come on inside them. They glowed. I loved the boys; I would learn to tolerate the dogs. I sacrificed two plastic bowls to the feeding and watering of the unexpected little guests .

Then, something strange began to happen. As I watched the boys play with Buck and Buster, I began to think them a little bit cute. I already thought the boys were cute. I'm talking about the dogs. They were mischievous and highly intelligent. I became convinced these exceptional dogs could learn to read and do multiplication.

Within a few hours, I found myself looking out the back window and smiling. "Just look at them chase each other. They really are cute little bundles of energy. They remind me of two little boys I know." My wonderful husband constructed a make-shift house. We gathered blankets to keep them warm and chew toys to keep them happy. We planned a veterinarian visit. I stopped tolerating them and started liking them.

By the next morning, I was a dog person. It was an overnight conversion. I woke up and raced out back to get a look at those little canine darlings. Had they slept well? Were they okay? Did they need me to start a college fund for them? Incidentally, please don't write saying I should have let the little dears stay inside. I said I liked them. I didn't say they should stay in the guest room like Aunt Sarah.

It's funny. I didn't think I was a dog person. My first impression of the little pups was less than admirable. I wanted to walk away from them. But I was wrong. There was something incredibly wonderful about Buck and Buster. I just had to give them a chance. Some of you already knew that. You love animals. Maybe it's people you have issue with. Come to think of it, there's a lesson here that could be applied to people. I could expound upon it but I trust you to figure it out. Be open to change. You may find yourself loving someone you never thought you could.

Ever Had a Perfect Day?

Ever had a perfect day? I did. Well, kind of. Yesterday was unseasonably cool and comfortable. My boys and I decided to go on a long trail walk through the woods. It was glorious. The two adventurous boys—sticks in hand—were followed by the two adventurous dogs—tails wagging in the cool breeze. Adventurous Mom was following along behind. We should have gotten it all on tape. The boys were playing so sweetly. The dogs were so very happy. I was imparting parental wisdom of every kind to my little charges as we bounded through the forest. My boys are still young enough to think I'm very smart......not as smart as Dad, but smart, nonetheless. We saw caterpillars and squirrels. The birds were singing sweetly in the trees. Ah, the sheer bliss of summer. I said to myself, "The boys will never forget this moment." We talked about the beautiful woods and how much we enjoy country life.

As though the blessings couldn't come fast enough, we came upon a creek bed filled with sand. We all sat down and set out to build some sand castles. This was the life. A mom and two boys building sand castles while two happy dogs played nearby. In the background, I think I heard Julie Andrews singing "The Sound of Music."

Then it happened! Out of nowhere, a yellow jacket came shooting up my older son's shirt. We stripped the shirt as he wailed in pain. He jumped and cried and the perfect day was ruined as the underside of his arm started swelling from the sting. "Oh, Honey, I'm so sorry," I said. As he was crying he said, "I can't stand these woods and that creek and I don't like living in the country." Okay. He's in recovery. I understand. As we headed back toward the house, one of the dogs began to yelp. It seems a yellow jacket had found him, too, and was stinging a sensitive spot on his rear end. I did what I could to help the poor dog when my younger son started screaming at the top of his lungs. Two yellow jackets were attacking his neck; his face was as red as a homegrown tomato. What's even worse is that he started doing that silent cry. You know the one I'm talking about. No noise—just a wide open mouth. Give him a few seconds. It's what I call the "I just fell off the porch" cry. You hear the thud and everyone waits for the wailing to begin. Finally, the wailing started. I picked him up. He, too, said that country life is not what it's cracked up to be...and he NEVER wants to go on the stupid trail again. So much for the perfect day.

It started out great. Happy mom. Happy kids. Happy dogs. Within an hour, the scene had changed. The unhappy mom was carrying the unhappy 6-year-old while the unhappy 8-year-old limped along saying encouraging things like, "We'll NEVER get home. It is TOO far and we are in TOO much pain to be out here hiking." Meanwhile, the dog began to limp helplessly as though his rear end were totally numb. Finally, the dog lay down in the middle of the trail—ready to give up the ghost. I was ready to join him. I was going to have to walk home carrying a 6-year-old, a paralyzed dog, and listening to an 8-year-old talk about what a terrible life he has. Julie Andrews stopped singing.

We made it home. We're all fine. Life goes on. Of course, there's a moral to the story. On this earth, there's not going to be a perfect day. Some are pretty close....but, perfect? No. Perfect is for another world. I can hardly wait.

Wanted: Cat Therapist

Does anyone know of a good cat therapist? We might even be willing to travel to a neighboring state. Please call or e-mail me post haste. We've been cat owners for less than 48 hours...and we've already permanently scarred the feline psyche of our new pet. Here's the unabridged story. It may not be appropriate for small children and by all means, don't read this column aloud...if you have a cat within earshot.

Our younger son has wanted a cat since birth. He was born a "cat person." We've tried to fulfill this desire with all myriad of stuffed cats, cat coloring books, cat video tapes, educational books about cats, three unruly male dogs, one unruly brother, two fun-loving parents. But, no. We knew the "cat thing" had reached a new level when he was found on his knees, hands clasped, saying, "God, please just send us a cat. Please just find me one little cat to love." I know. Get a tissue. Providence was clearly on his side.

My husband and I recently had to travel to a funeral in Middle Tennessee and we made the mistake of leaving our children overnight with "friends." Everyone knows that REAL friends would never expose another person's child to a living breathing animal in need of a home. I thought this was written in a "friendship handbook" somewhere. Remind me to write and circulate the handbook. Our younger son greeted us as though he'd just seen the Publisher's Clearinghouse van..."They have a cat they want to give us. No, really! Can you BELIEVE it, Mom? Isn't this the greatest thing? God answered my prayer!!" Yeah. Trust me. I can hardly believe it.

A few days later found us traveling home from our friends' house with two happy boys in the backseat holding a solid black male cat they affectionately called "Ninja." The lesson? Don't try to fight Providence.

I told the boys to put Ninja in the cardboard box and I would carry the box onto the porch. But Ninja heard the barking of our three dogs and jumped out of the box and headed for the woods. Buddy, our golden retriever/collie, had little Ninja "treed" within three seconds. That's when it hit me. Dogs and cats are only friends in Disney movies. All of us ran to the tree and coaxed Ninja down while my older son held back Buddy. The moment Ninja's paws hit the ground, he raced deep into the woods. His place in the "rural" food chain was becoming clear.

I don't know much about cats. So we ran through the woods chasing after little Ninja. Yes, I know. Never run after a cat. It doesn't work. I surely could have used that advice a few days ago. Providence had taken a terrible turn.

My younger son could hardly sleep that night as he sorrowfully wept the loss of this little feline he had owned for less than an hour. There were no words of comfort. Again, he prayed, "God, you know where Ninja is. Please help him get home."

The next morning came. No Ninja. That afternoon at about 2:00 I noticed a hobbling little prodigal cat peering through the woods. My heart jumped. I didn't want another night of weeping from my younger charge. I was a "mama on a mission." Running outside with a big white laundry basket and a bowl of cat food, I determined to "capture" the escaped feline, if it killed me. And it almost did. I didn't realize that when a fat woman runs through the woods carrying a laundry basket and yelling, "Here Kitty, Kitty" at the top of her lungs...it's a grave health risk. I finally used a top-secret psychological ploy to lure the coveted cat into the laundry basket. Ah. The thrill of victory.

Ninja was captured and he's happily at home in the enclosed back porch. But I'm not sure he trusts us. All of us have learned some valuable lessons through the experience. Country dogs who spend their free time chasing squirrels and chewing on deer carcasses don't tend to socialize well with felines. Life is a great adventure. And by all means, never run after a cat.

Life Lessons from a Stupid Dog

Every newspaper columnist in America needs a stupid dog. This is an absolute requirement. What's that? Smart dogs? No, smart dogs won't work. Smart dogs are neither funny nor even remotely entertaining to read about. No one wants to read about a dog that fetches, behaves, and lies quietly by the fire. See? You almost fell asleep reading just one sentence about a smart and obedient dog. Plus, there is something rather braggadocios about owning a smart dog. It's kind of like saying, "My kid is smarter than your kid." No one wants to read about dogs that have been blessed with superior abilities. Stupid dogs, on the other hand, provide rich and rewarding writing opportunities. I have been blessed. Truly blessed.

We have two dogs. One is medium-sized and mildly stupid. The other is quite large and profoundly stupid. A few months ago, our biggest stupidest dog broke my husband's arm. No. I didn't pay the dog a finder's fee, even though I did glean a whole column from the incident. I have a feeling I'll have to start a tab. Within the last 24 hours, this beast has dragged my pot of front porch petunias into the woods and eaten them for breakfast. He has knocked one of the trash cans over and licked the inside of 3 Ragu spaghetti sauce jars while shredding an empty bacon package and depositing the remains on the front sidewalk. A combination of disobedience and lack of intelligence has rendered him a plethora of potential column material.

But two stupid dogs weren't enough for my animal lovin' family. Oh no. The free pet opportunities just kept on a comin'. Believe it or not, all of our pets were given to us free of charge. Yeah. Wonders never cease.

We became cat owners a few months ago. This, too, provided a newspaper column because the cat got lost in the woods and I had to hire an out-of-state cat therapist to help him handle the trauma. OK. Not really. The cat did get lost, but I passed on the cat therapist.

On the day our big stupid dog met our new cat, the whole family feared tragedy. After all, the dog's large jaws could quickly snuff out the very life of this little 3 lb. kitty. But, no. Brains are more powerful than brawn, my friend. More powerful than brawn. When our 70 lb. black lab/mutt/four-legged beast came bounding down the front lawn toward the kitty, I reached to rescue the poor little feline. No rescue was needed. Our cat, aptly named Ninja, began his psychological dog torture. The performance of a lifetime! Ninja hissed. He flung his back up in a bow while making a strange gurgling sound. I thought sure he was going to speak Chinese, pull some num-chucks out of the azalea bush, and proceed toward an out and out doggy whoopin'. But, alas, his show of dominance was enough to make the great beast run scared.

So many life lessons are found in our daily interaction with animals. Here are just a few. Even stupid folks, I mean animals, can be loveable. Confidence and attitude often make up for lack of physical strength. Pets are usually happy and rarely need therapy. Besides, if I were going to hire a therapist, it would be for a woman who has two mud-covered little boys, two stupid dogs, an emotionally disturbed cat, and shredded garbage all over the front lawn.

Chapter 8

The Battle of the Bulge: Fighting the Fat Monster

It's Spring and I'm Still Fat

The birds are singing. The flowers are blooming. There's only one little problem. I'm still fat. The layers of clothing are coming off. But, there are some layers that don't seem to be budging. I love fall and winter. Oh sure. I always say things like, "I love fall because of the beautiful colors." "Snow makes everything look fresh and clean." But, who am I kidding? I love fall and winter because the layers of clothing hide my own little layers. Winter means sweaters and jackets and boots.

Spring means shorts with funny named colors like honeydew melon. Yeah. That's a prophecy fulfilled as far as I'm concerned. When I put on my honeydew melon shorts and my watermelon sleeveless shirt, I'm the complete melon. Believe me. I'm not even going to make jokes about the sleeveless shirt. They've all been made. Sleeveless shirts are the enemy. They injure people and must be battled against at all costs.

Every winter I make strange little arrangements with myself concerning my weakness.
"This is it. By spring, I'll be feeling fresher, lighter, younger, more alive. I may even run a triathlon." It's April. I'm holding out one last hope for a 2-3 month cold snap, but that seems doubtful.

It's not about vanity or appearance. It's about health. Okay. It may be a little about vanity or appearance. But, predominantly it's about health and about overcoming weakness in my life. I'm not going to live in the regrets of the past. I'm starting fresh.

I'm 40 years old. I'm not chubby or chunky. I'm fat. I'm facing the facts and deciding to do something about it. SO,

I'm asking you to give me a hand here. I need some accountability. I've decided I want to shed quite a few pounds. I've opted to steer clear of the "eat ½ cow daily and no bagels" method. I've decided instead to go with what's now considered the archaic method. I'm going to eat a little less and move a little more. The way I figure it, I've been eating more than my body needs for fuel. My body has been storing this fuel in inconvenient little places just waiting for a famine. This is not rocket science. I eat too much.

I've made the decision. Here's where you come in. I'm giving you, the reader, the right to call me down if you find me eating something that seems "inappropriate." SO, here's what you're looking for. I drive a 4 door red Saturn with Weakley County tags. Be on the lookout. I've been known to drift into neighboring counties. If I'm at Dairy Queen, be sure the kids are with me and only 2 kid cones get purchased. Feel free to make a citizen's arrest. Do a search of the car, if you have to.

IF you see me at a local grocery store, take liberty to check the cart for contraband. Be suspicious of the following items: Little Debbie anything, chocolate in any form, and Lorna Doones. Yeah. I know. Few people even know what Lorna Doones are. They're the undiscovered quintessential shortbread cookies. I digress. I fully realize that some people can handle these wonderful foods in moderation. I'm just not one of them. So, I'm asking you to come up to the cart and say, "Drop it, Lisa!" Be aware. In a moment of weakness I may cop an excuse, "I've got kids. They crave sweets." Don't buy it. My kids love fruit. Hang tough. Remember, my health is at stake here. Repeat after me, "Drop it, Lisa!" And if you see me walking briskly through your neighborhood, shout out, "You GO GIRL!" If you see me walking briskly through your neighborhood while eating a Snickers bar, remember the phrase, "Drop it, Lisa!"

I'm under no illusion that this will be an easy journey. I'm asking God for help. And I'll be checking in with you from time to time. I'll let you know how things are going. Will some of you join me? Write me and we'll travel the journey to better health together! I promise to write you back. If you have a weakness for food, your confession is safe with me. Trust me. I understand. I also need to keep a sense of humor through the process. You can help me with that, too. Maybe we'll start a West Tennessee Health Revolution!

I'm hyped! I feel like Jared on the Subway commercials. I hear Disney music in the background. This is the first day of the rest of my life. I feel like running slow motion through a field of wildflowers wearing my honeydew melon shorts and my watermelon sleeveless shirt. On second thought, maybe I'll wait on that.

Fat and Frugal Folks in the Buffet Line

All-you-can-eat buffets are a danger zone for me. I'm petitioning the national government to place large signs at every public buffet line in this great country of ours. The sign could be propped up next to the croutons and would simply read: "Warning: Buffet lines can be hazardous to your health. If you believe macaroni is a vegetable, step away from the sneeze guard."

Fat people. God bless us. I promise we're trying. All-you-can-eat buffets are just too much for us to bear. Somehow we've grown to crave foods that are less than healthy for our bodies. I laugh when people say, "I'm craving a salad." Or "Can I have fruit on the side instead of fries?" Yeah. Fruit and salad. I've always wanted to say at lunchtime, "Gee whiz, get that nasty cheeseburger away from me. I'm craving mandarin orange slices and a head of lettuce." And while we're on the subject of salad, I'd like to state my opinion regarding fat free dressing. America has gone totally awry on this subject. Fat free dressing is like saying, "tall short people." Look up the word "dressing" in the dictionary. No. Don't even bother. You can trust me on this one. The definition of dressing: a creamy, yummy concoction made of buttermilk, mayonnaise, and a Ranch dressing packet.

But, there's something far, far worse than just being a fat person at an all-you-can-eat buffet. Oh my, yes. My propensity for indulging in mass carbohydrates is not the only danger area. Frugality is my other hazard in the buffet line. Frugal people love to pay little and get a lot. We're bargain hunters, sale shoppers. We love nothing more than feeling like we discovered the deal of the century. That's why all-you-can-eat buffets are recipes for disaster for us. We'd love nothing better than to prove we can pay $6.99 for something

143

and receive $15.00 worth. Again, I'm calling for government regulations. Perhaps just a small sign which reads: "Warning: If you've ever taken home the leftover ketchup packets from fast food restaurants and placed them in the door of your refrigerator, step away from the buffet."

Oh friends, life is full of temptations, am I right? The following test may be painful for some of you. Please answer the next few questions as honestly as possible. This will help you determine whether you need to stay away from the all-you-can-eat buffet. Have you ever ordered water and used lemon packets and Sweet'N Low to make lemonade and then congratulated yourself for saving $1.75? Have you ever chosen to eat at a Mexican restaurant because of the free tortilla chips? Have you ever eaten more than two bowls of the free tortilla chips? Have you ever gone somewhere for breakfast and wished they offered free tortilla chips? Have you ever poured the free salsa into the change purse of your wallet? There. There. No need for crying. I'm not calling you a bad person. I'm not throwing stones. I'm just saying it would probably be best for you to order from the menu. This will shield you from the temptation of eating three bowls of ice cream and filling your purse with sunflower seeds from the salad bar. I am friend, not foe.

Now for a quick re-cap. Fat free dressing is not dressing. Macaroni is not a vegetable. And if you find yourself craving mandarin oranges and a head of lettuce, count your blessings.

Temptation at the Checkout Line

The grocery store checkout line. We all have to push our carts through that infamous tunnel of temptation. Some of you are morbidly drawn to reading about whether Britney Spears is expecting David Letterman's baby. Magazines which feature Britney Spears are a tragic waste of trees, in my estimation. And if Richard Simmons and Dionne Warwick really did tie the knot in Vegas, I'm not remotely interested in who was best man or what the wedding cake looked like. Then there's always a baby from Greenland who was born with a dinosaur head. I don't know. Somehow it doesn't seem right to gawk at people from Greenland who look like dinosaurs. I'm almost positive my mom once told me, "Sweetie, never gawk at dinosaur people from Greenland. It's not polite." Celebrity magazines just don't jump out and grab me.

Marketers have figured this out and now they offer a whole plethora of product choices in the checkout line. Lint rollers. Bleach pens. Hand sanitizer. Doggie treats. Duct tape. Massage oil. Yes, massage oil. Massage oil is right next to the duct tape. I 'm confused. I don't know whether to plan a romantic dinner or crawl under the house and patch a leaky pipe. And lip balm? You can find lip balm of every description in the checkout line. I saw a TV show recently about people who are addicted to lip balm. Yes, I'm dead serious. If you have a lip balm addiction, avoid the checkout line at all cost. Hire a personal shopper.

I rarely experience an uncontrollable urge to buy a lint roller or a big roll of duct tape. There's only ONE thing that gets my attention in the ol' checkout line. Chocolate. Chocolate. Chocolate. I go through the same mental exercises every time I approach the checkout line. It's an inner dialogue with my conscience that goes something like this:

"Boy, a 3 Musketeers bar would sure hit the spot right now."

"Lisa, forget it. You don't need a 3 Musketeers bar."

"It's less than 200 calories."

"Lisa, get real. It will go straight to your behind. Put it back. Put it back, I say."

"Look, it's just one candy bar. It can't hurt. Besides, I did three miles on the treadmill today."

"Lisa, you did that three miles to eliminate the two baskets of tortilla chips from Tuesday. Girlfriend, you're working on what's in storage, not what's still on the loading dock. And besides, people are watching you. They're saying, 'Look at the fat girl buying a 3 Musketeers bar that's going right to her behind.'"

"No, they think I'm buying it for one of my kids."

"Who are you kidding, Lisa? They know. Every person within a ten mile radius knows there's a fat girl buying a candy bar in checkout line 7. Trust me. I'm your conscience. Put the candy back and read about Brad and Angelina."

"Brad and Angelina are boring. I want the chocolate."

And so the conversation goes. Sometimes the forces of good win out. Other times the evil chocolate voice overtakes my sensibilities. Either way, it's an indicator that marketers know what we're thinking. And that's a scary thought. Oh, and if you see me in checkout line 7 with a candy bar in my hand, feel free to do a loving intervention. Slowly put the chocolate back, hand me a cherry lip balm, and hope for the best.

I Love Swimsuit Season

I want to thank all the male readers out there who have faithfully read this column and supported me with your comments, e-mails, and encouragement. But I'm giving you the week off. This is the first column I've ever written that I truly think is a "woman only" subject.

Women, let's talk. Hot weather has arrived. The pools have opened. It's swimsuit season. For those of you who have yet to don a swimsuit, I'm reaching out to hold your hand. It's okay. I'm going to walk you through this. Go to the store of your choice. Don't linger at the jewelry counter or dilly dally over the purses. You're on a mission. Hold your head high and walk proudly to the swimsuit section. If a sales person offers to assist you, smile and say with incredible confidence, "I'm here on a swimsuit mission." If you have a lot of things that need to be supported, by all means look for one of those suits that holds everything in place. I think the suit I bought was engineered by the Germans responsible for Mercedes-Benz. There's genius in the engineering. Getting into the suit takes about 45 minutes; but once I'm in, nothing moves. Make sure everything is nicely covered and contained. Buy the least offensive suit you can find. Take it home. Clip the tags. Eat a healthy and balanced diet. Walk or exercise almost every day. And move on with your life.

I love swimsuit season. It's uncomfortable and it's humbling. Humility is not a bad thing. My kids love to go to the pool. I love to go with them.

I want to share this swimsuit story I read in a magazine once: A "less than perfect" mom had kids who were always asking her to go swimming. She hated the thought of putting on a swimsuit. She kept putting them off and putting them off.

"This is ridiculous," she said. "My kids want to go to the beach and I should love them enough to take them." SO, she donned a swimsuit and went to the beach with her children. They played. They swam. They had a great time. Her comment: "I ran down the beach in my less than perfect body and my new swimsuit and y'know what happened? Nothing."

I love it!! Everything she had dreaded about swimsuit season was all just a paper tiger. Nobody cared.

Let's make a vow together, girlfriends. Let's hug people. Let's love people. Let's play with our kids. But let's stop obsessing about wearing a swimsuit or about having pasty white legs. I speak from experience. I have two things working against me. The chubby legs are one thing, but my complexion is a shade lighter than school glue. I've decided to steer clear of the sun in honor of my desire to actually live a long life. (Excessive sun exposure can cause skin cancer. It also causes premature aging. I'm interested in avoiding both of those, if possible.) A few years ago I decided to rebel against that knowledge and soak up the sun. I came home with a reddish version of a tan. My dear husband who has often warned me of the dangers of skin cancer said, "Sweetie, don't make me have to call in the friends and family to do a 'tanning intervention.' You need to steer clear of the sun."

Okay. I'm white and chubby. There are more profound issues in the world. I've already been to the pool several times and nobody's life seemed radically changed by my presence. My kids thought it was great fun to play in the water with Mom. The earth is still spinning on its axis. All is right with the world. Swimsuit season is here. I feel like a run down the beach.

Fall Fashion Felonies

I watched a New York City fashion show on the Today show this morning. I've always been the upwardly mobile sort who likes to stay informed on what I should be wearing on my afternoon outings to Wal-Mart or the elementary school. And the fashion show didn't disappoint. Inspiring. First, the bad news. No offense, but some of you are committing fashion felonies every day in this fine area of the country. You're wearing matching colors. You're wearing clothes that fit appropriately. Your hems are even. Some of you are even dressing for comfort AND combing your hair. Tsk. Tsk. And those garden-friendly rubber clog shoes with the alligator name? Let me fill you in. They're not wearing those on the runways of New York City. Shame. Shame. Shame.

Now that I'm enlightened, I'm more than willing to share my fashion expertise with the rest of you. Feel free to take notes. Fall fashion is all about "layering." Fashion experts on the show talked about "layering" this and "layering" that. After watching the last model exit the runway, I knew what I had to do. Someone had to stand up and be a trend setter. I immediately walked into the guest room, removed the paisley bedspread from the queen-size bed, and draped my tall fat body in the layers. Grabbing my son's Tae Kwon Do belt, I cinched the bedspread and completed the "look."

Knowing that "attitude" is the key to fall fashion, I held my head high while strutting down to the outdoor shed where I found the necessary accessories. Those of us "in the know" understand that accessorizing is an essential part of fall style. After cutting an appropriate portion of leftover chain with a wire cutter, I realized I had the perfect necklace accessory for the bedspread ensemble. I was looking good and feeling confident. A freshly washed, faded red, oil rag adorned my neck as the "unmatched" scarf. I was ready to take the bull by the horns.

Before I left the house, I took one more glance into the bathroom mirror. I tossed my hair back and forth until it stood straight up as though I had been awakened in the middle of the night by a train coming through the living room. Finally, I plastered a deep frown on my face as though the train had run over my big toe. Frowning and messed up hair are modeling essentials. I know. I saw the fashion show, remember? Other than the fact that I can eat my weight in biscuits and gravy, I was feeling like a fashion model. Yes sirree. I was ready to venture into carpool line with style.

That's when I realized I had not yet adorned my feet with stylish footwear. All the New York City models wore high-heel pumps. But by this time, I was tired. My resistance was lowering. And that's when I saw them. Shining like a bright light from heaven. There on the very top of the shoe rack were those lovely ever-comfortable green garden-friendly rubber clogs with the alligator name. Pure comfort. Pure unadulterated foot heaven. No. I couldn't veer off course. No. Don't do it. "Don't do it," I whispered to myself. But it was too late. Before my brain could direct my body, the wide ugly rubber shoes were adorning my size 10 feet. Ahh.

Then came the epiphany. There are women in New York City who wear pumps and don't eat gravy. They're frowning. There are women in rural America who eat gravy and wear comfortable shoes. We're smiling.

Fat Girl Joins the Gym

I did it. I joined the gym. The world is my oyster. I have a new lease on life. It's as though I have drunk from the fountain of youth. I'm serious. The minute fat people start working out, they feel miraculously thinner. After the first work-out I came home and said, "Honey, look how thin I look in these pants! They're nearly falling off of me. It's a miracle. I'm a wisp of my former self. I should consider a career in modeling." It was euphoria, pure and simple. People who are in shape have been telling us fat people this for years. "Work out. You'll feel better." "Work out. You'll be healthier." "Work out. You'll live longer." "Work out. We're tired of watching your jelly belly jiggle." No more. Move over, skinny folk. Fat people are on the move.

Some people naively wonder why I hadn't joined the gym before now. They're thinking, "Lisa, you're fat. Why aren't you doing something about it?" Tsk. Tsk. Tsk. There's always a critic. I have a perfectly reasonable explanation for my behavior. I didn't want to join the gym until I lost weight. I'm serious. That's been holding me back for years. I say things like, "The minute I drop 40 pounds, I'm gonna get my fine lookin' self into some bright red spandex and down to the gym I will go." What's that? You say that doesn't make sense? What do you mean, it doesn't make sense? Oh friend, there are a lot of things in this life that don't make sense. Sugar-free pudding. Bright lights in store fitting rooms. Anti-aging cream. Yard dwarfs. Liquid meals. Infomercials for spray-on hair. I could go on and on. Perhaps we should all hold our criticism, yes?

When fat people decide to start working out, it's a detailed process. First, there was the "humiliation phase." This involved putting on sweat pants. Even skinny people look bigger in sweat pants. It makes us fat people so "fluffy" that we look like one of those big balloons in the Macy's Thanksgiving Day parade. Part 2 of the "humiliation phase" involved going down to the work-out facility while wearing the sweat pants. I went through the front door and said, "I'm a fat felon. And I'm here to surrender." I was glad they didn't put me in handcuffs and frisk me for Little Debbie contraband. That was a gracious act of mercy.

But the "humiliation phase" was nothing compared to the "mortal fear phase." The "mortal fear phase" began when they looked at me and said, "Let's hop on the scales, shall we?" That's when the room started spinning and I had to think quickly before I spoke. "This may be hard to believe, but I'm allergic to public scales. I'm serious. It's a horrible childhood malady. Yeah, there should be a little thing I carry with me, like people who are allergic to bee stings." They didn't buy it. Through in-depth therapy, I've blocked the next few moments from my memory. All I remember is standing on the scales in a fog and whispering the words, "I'm 6 feet tall and big for my age."

After the "mortal fear phase" comes the "irrational optimism phase." This is the glorious reward for putting on sweat pants and getting on the scales. The "irrational optimism phase" basically convinced me that in a matter of months I'd be one of those people on the cover of a national magazine holding out my old fat pants. And I choose to embrace that notion. After all, I'm already a wisp of my former self.

Chapter 9

Rural America: Embracing Yard Dwarfs

Cotton Pickin' as an Educational Tool

I'm getting older. I know I'm getting older because I use sentences that start with, "Back when I was a kid..."

I come up with all sorts of facts that were true "back then." When I went to school, we didn't start until September. When I was young, school supplies consisted of a notebook, paper, and a pencil. When I was a young girl, a computer was a bulldozer-sized piece of machinery in a warehouse in California.

When I was in elementary school, no one had ever heard of a dry-erase marker. We used old-fashioned chalk and erasers. Sure, our lungs filled with chalk dust and the room had a yellowish tint to it. The privilege of good behavior was that you got to take those chalky erasers outside and beat them together, filling your lungs with even more chalk dust. Okay. Maybe it wasn't the best system. But, have you ever smelled a dry-erase marker? Pregnant women shouldn't come within ten feet of that thing.

Life has changed over the years. That's usually a good thing. But not all change is good. I fear that my kids' generation lacks the discipline, work ethic, and attention span of former generations. This concerns me, but I have a solution to the dilemma.

Some of you have lived long enough to remember when school was dismissed for cotton pickin'. I'm not quite that old, but I must admit it's a pretty bright idea for present day academia. Hear me out. I'm not talking about missing weeks and weeks of valuable academic instruction time. I'm just talkin' about a few days of "instruction" of a different nature.

I think parents and teachers will rally around the idea once they hear my brilliant plan. My kids (and I suspect all kids) have a tendency to whine and complain about little inconveniences like math homework and limited recess. I think a little cotton pickin' would be just what the doctor ordered. A miracle cure.

My plan would begin with the teachers enthusiastically announcing, "Hey kids! For the next few days, you'll have no homework assignments, no math problems, and no reading time. We're taking a few days off for cotton pickin'. You'll not even be eating in the school cafeteria. Let's just say you'll be having your meals 'picnic style'."

Oh the cheers that would resonate from the mouths of school children everywhere. "YAY! No school!" they would naively say to each other. "COOL! We're gonna ditch these math books...and pick cotton!" Yeah. You surely are.

On the first morning, all the kids would meet at the cotton fields at 6:00 a.m. I think it would be wise to have an old man who has extensive military training to be in charge of the first day's pickin'. Lunch would be cold water and pinto beans. Whining would result in an extra hour of work. The second day's pickin' would be much the same. The third day would consist of a choice. Teachers would stand in the middle of the field and simply ask, "Anybody want a ride to school for some math drills?" The fields would empty in a New York minute. Children everywhere would approach their education with renewed fervor, appreciation, and excitement. I can see it now. It would be a revolution.

Revolutionaries are always treated with suspicion at first. SO, until I can sell my plan to the general public, you'll find my boys taking out the trash and cleaning bathrooms here at home. And as always, whining earns more work.

Lost on Tennessee Back Roads

A professional fisherman was once asked, "Isn't it scary trying to make a living by fishing?"

His reply, "Not really. It's about confidence. I'm confident I can go out on that lake and catch a really big fish. And usually I do."

That settles it. I need a professional fisherman to ride shot gun each time I'm on the back roads of Tennessee. I'm experiencing a crisis of confidence. When I get lost, the professional fisherman could say something encouraging like, "Lisa, this road is full of turns. But, you know which ones to take. You are a confident and capable driver. You are not directionally-challenged. You are woman. Hear you roar."

We're rural people now. We're blessed that our boys have made friends with rural people. This means people invite us over who live "out from" places. I know I'm in trouble when someone types a page of directions for me and says, "You'll have no problem, I'm sure. We just live "out from " Dukedom. It could be Sidonia or Como or Rives. But, it's that term "out from" that's especially scary to someone like me who gets lost in Wal-Mart parking lots. When someone says they live "out from" an unincorporated town that doesn't have a Dairy Queen or a pay phone, be afraid. Be very afraid. Call the nearest professional fisherman.

Here are some words of wisdom for those of you who are trying to follow directions to someone's house who lives "out from "a small town. Take heed to my warnings.

156

#1. Never drink a lot of coffee on the day of the journey. You don't need the caffeine-induced jitters on those hair pin curves. Excessive caffeine can also make you more prone to yell, "Boys, I'm going to put you out in that cornfield if you don't stop pounding those plastic Power Rangers against the window! I'm serious! I'm at the breaking point!" Here's another reason to lay low on the coffee consumption. There are no bathrooms in the middle of nowhere. Trust me. When you get lost in the middle of nowhere, look around. There is no port-a-potty.

#2. Never start crying. Once the crying starts, the self-degrading comments are soon to follow, "MY WORD! Why don't I know which way South is? WHY can't I find Hwy. 97? WHY have I passed that same silver silo three times?"

#3. Be cautious of local directions. Local people are prone to say things like, "Stay on this road till you get to Charlie and Inez's place. Turn right by Charlie's new woodshop and go all the way down to old man Simpson's place. Turn left when you see the field of Peaches n Cream corn right across from Aunt Charlene's trailer. If Aunt Charlene is out on the porch, don't forget to wave. She's always been kinda sensitive. Go past the cornfield until you get to the old schoolhouse. The road you're looking for is about 5 miles south of the old schoolhouse. If you pass Bo Bo's silver silo, you'll know you've gone the wrong way." Pass me a tissue. I need a good cry.

#4. People assume that if I arrive at the destination, I'm now home free. Nothing could be further from the truth. For a directionally-challenged person, arriving is only half the battle. Let me put it this way. If I had a hard time following the written directions when everything on the page was in the right order, what would POSSIBLY make people think I could follow the directions once everything on the page is completely backward? I know. Good point. And if I just back track, I'll be on a silver silo sight-seeing tour again. I rarely have enough tissues for that.

I love rural life. I understand why people like living ten miles south of nowhere. Just be patient with me. When you invite me to your "out from" house, allow an extra 30 minutes for my journey. And tell Aunt Charlene to put on a pot of coffee and be on the look-out. I may need a break about half way there.

Fairs, Festivals, and Fine Country Livin'

I'm addicted to rural life. New York City has Broadway. Chicago has the Cubs. Los Angeles has the smog. But, only rural America has pickle contests, bean cook-offs, and dog shows where the dogs possess real talent. I've seen those high and mighty dog shows on TV. Downright boring. Dog hair stylists. Fancy papers. I've yet to see one of those TV dogs actually do anything that resembles real talent. Come to a small-town dog show and you'll find a dog willing to dress up in jeans, a bandana, and a cowboy hat. You'll see dogs who aren't ashamed to eat funnel cakes and engage in a few standard canine tricks. No funnel cakes or cowboy hats allowed in those fancy dog shows. And they call that entertainment? Embarrassingly narrow-minded. They need to come to a small town fair or festival and broaden their horizons.

I didn't realize rural life had taken such a strong hold on me until I celebrated my birthday recently. The morning of my birthday my romantic husband surprised me by informing me that he had acquired a babysitter and was prepared to take me to a swanky Jackson eating establishment to celebrate 42 years of living. I could see the scene in my mind. A lovely restaurant. Romantic atmosphere. Candles aglow. Dressed as though we were going to a funeral, we'd be holding hands across the table and sharing special memories. The bill would come and we'd see a week's worth of grocery money up in smoke...all in honor of my birth. As the beautiful plans went swirling around in my head, one predominant thought kept coming to the forefront of my mind....the soybean. The soybean? What was I thinking? HOW could I be thinking about the Soybean Festival when the offer of a lovely evening of fine dining lay within my grasp? Welcome to rural America.

My husband returned home that afternoon ready to shower and put on the necessary funeral clothes. I met him at the door and said, "Honey, I love you. Thanks for planning such a special evening in honor of my birthday. Most women would swoon at the idea of a romantic restaurant with a good lookin' guy. I'm not sure how to break this to you. Well. Y'see, it's that…well, rural life has kind of taken hold of me, y'know? Honey, it's gotten to me. It has. I crave cornbread and milk. I read the Electric Co-Op magazine cover to cover. I listen to the weather as though my life depends on the weather. Honey, I'm a country girl. Pure and simple. The happiest birthday I can imagine would be going with you to the Soybean Festival. We could take the lawn chairs and sit out under the stars enjoying a free concert. We'd see people we know. You could even buy me a lemonade and a funnel cake. How's that sound?" Knowing there would be no uncomfortable funeral clothes involved in the new plan, he just smiled.

The birthday went off without a hitch. We dropped $12 at a local small-town eatery. We caught the end of the radio-sponsored Price is Right game. We walked around and saw many folks we knew. It was a grand way to spend a birthday. When people inquired where our boys were and we told them of the babysitter, they said, "You're on a DATE at the Soybean Festival?" Of course. Where else?

That night we sat under the stars in our lawn chairs and listened to the concert. At one point, the love of my life grabbed my hand, looked into my eyes, and said, "Honey, are you having a happy birthday?" With the wafting smell of funnel cakes in the air and the presence of a good man beside me, the reply was obvious. "I can't think of any place I'd rather be."

Life Lessons from the Waltons

Remember "The Waltons"? Our family recently watched a DVD of the first season of this iconic TV series. It was pure joy to watch our boys discovering the family which had been such a part of our lives growing up. Jim Bob. Mary Ellen. Little Elizabeth with her flaming red hair. Grandma Walton with her callous outer coating which hid her tender center. Such a beautiful picture of rural life. The Walton family has provided valuable lessons for our children, too. The value of a dollar. The difficulties of the depression. The stability of a loving home.

I always get emotional when the camera turns to restless John Boy writing in his journal each night. He respected his parents, completed farm chores, and ate cornbread and pinto beans. He even laughed at Grandpa's jokes. But John Boy had a secret. He knew he couldn't stay on Walton's mountain. His destiny lay elsewhere. There was no stopping him. He was born for something "out there."

Torn between the quiet country life and the life he believes awaits him on the other side of Walton's mountain, John Boy learns to live in the balance. He learns to appreciate the rural foundation of his life, without forsaking his dreams. His parents learn some lessons, too. Some people are born to move away. There's nothing we can do about it, and we shouldn't even try.

Mama and Daddy always told me there were two kinds of people. Pillars and movers. Thankfully, they taught me great respect for both parties. My grandparents were pillars. Granny and Pappa lived in the same house on the same West Kentucky farm for more than 50 years. They attended the same church. They knew the same people. Granny fried apples the same way in the same kind of skillet in the same kitchen for more than half a century. Their small rural community would have been drastically different had they not been there. Summer evenings found them snapping green beans on the back porch. "Sure was hot today." "Oh, and doesn't the garden look dry." "Aunt Lucille called and said Imogene has taken to her bed. I'll carry some beans and a coconut cake over tomorrow." If my grandparents wanted a different life, we never knew it. They were the picture of contentment. I think they were born to be pillars.

My mama grew up on that same farm. Snapping beans. Frying apples. Making good grades. Respecting her parents. But she didn't want to stay. She couldn't stay. Like John Boy, she had a tremendous respect for the rural foundation of her life, while dreaming of a life "out there." A life she would eventually experience. Mama was a mover.

Pillars and movers are essential for every community. If we didn't have pillars, we would have no stability. If we didn't have movers, we would have no diversity. As I watch my two little boys don rubber boots and run through the woods outside our rural home, I begin to wonder. As adults, will they live down the road or will they live in Malaysia? Will they live in Como or New York City? We've no way of knowing. Regardless of where they land, I have a feeling they'll both remember the trail that leads down to the creek bed, the sound of crickets chirping on a summer night, and the warmth and joy of their childhood home. Good night, Stephen. Good night, Jonathan.

Country Church Homecomin'

If you've grown up in the rural south, you've more than likely been to a country church homecomin'. No. Not a homecoming. A homecomin'. If you say the word with a full "ing" sound, you haven't been to a real one. Recently, we were guests at a real homecomin' event. What a colorful picture of our rural heritage!

After a time of praise and worship, we gathered in the front church yard where we enjoyed a true "dinner on the grounds." Fried chicken. Homemade pie. Sweet tea. A cool breeze provided the perfect accompaniment to our outdoor time of fellowship. After the meal, we all went back inside for the sangin'. No. Not the singing. It was not a singing. It was a sangin'. Two wonderful local groups lifted their voices in song. Everyone sang. We raised the roof of the old country church singing beloved hymns that had passed from generation to generation. Unlike the "days of old" when a homecomin' event was a test of human endurance, we didn't stay all day and night. When it got about nap time, we all went home for the day.

The event brought guests of every description. Young people. Old people. Small children did cartwheels in the cool grass. Older people moved more slowly with the aid of a cane or a friend. People whose ancestors had once been members of the church came from neighboring towns. People whose relatives had been buried in the church cemetery were there. It was an annual pilgrimage back to the place where so much of their family history had unfolded. Weddings. Baptisms. Funerals. Being a part of the homecomin' celebration reminded me that there is value in family history. It reminded me that while some of us were born to be "movers," others were born to be "pillars" in a community. What were the "pillars" of this community like? Did they ever dream of moving away? Or were their hearts firmly fixed in Northwest Tennessee?

At one point, I walked over to the cemetery, placed my hands on the fence, and examined the names and dates on the headstones. What was life like more than 100 years ago when this church had been founded? When they rode in wagons to start this country church, what was their mission? Were they considered traditionalists or were they revolutionaries? For just a moment, I wished I had been there on the first Sunday of services. Headstones marked the graves of people who had been so instrumental in establishing vital communities, churches, families. Did they know that years and years later descendants and community folks would still be gathering for worship and dinner on the grounds? Did they realize small children would still be learning the words to "Rock of Ages" or "Holy, Holy, Holy?"

Homecomin' reminded me of the ever-important balance of life. Relishing and appreciating the past while embracing and engaging the future. Rejoicing in the heritage our forefathers passed down while being progressive in understanding a new generation of worshippers. Some things are destined to change. The life-changing message of love and grace remains the same.

Country Magazine is Off Course

Some things are just false advertising. False advertising, I tell ya. Two years ago, when my family and I moved to our rural home, a dear friend in Texas thought she gave me the perfect gift. A two-year subscription to "Country Home." After all, we bought a home. It was in the country. What could be a more perfect gift than a magazine called "Country Home"? What a sad disappointment for all.

I'm gonna let you West Tennesseans in on a little secret. Not everyone looks at the word "country" in the same way. Y'see, it didn't take me long to realize that the editors and contributors of this particular magazine were not exactly "country." Poor things. Most of them seem pretty city-savvy to me. Some of them even live in the city and "weekend" in the country. It has been my observation that these fine folks know nothing about real country living. It would be like me editing a Mathematics Journal. If you don't believe me, I'll be more than glad to share some examples of their rural naivety.

Here's an excerpt about a supposed "country designer" from the May 2006 issue, page 112: "In a world of faux finishes and pre-framed artwork, Danny's expressive, eco-chic style is refreshing-and in demand. As an eco-stylist and lifestyle consultant, his client roster includes the likes of Stella McCartney, Daryl Hannah, and the Kimpton Hotels."

OK. Back up the pick-up truck. First, I believe this fine magazine is making fun of the pre-framed artwork that REAL country folk often acquire from stores with the word dollar in the name. Second, I have never in my 42 years of living met an eco-stylist and lifestyle consultant in rural America. I'm not saying eco-stylists don't live in rural Dresden. I'm saying

I've never met one. In fact, I don't know one person in rural Dresden who designs homes or "lifestyles" for people like Daryl Hannah.

If you're not already convinced that this magazine is not exactly "country," here's another example. Page 106 of the February 2006 issue states the following regarding food:

"Risotto-the creamy, toothsome Northern Italian rice dish-is quintessential slow food. Contrary to popular belief, it's not arduous or time-consuming (only about 30 minutes total) but it is best when made in the traditional way with the right ingredients, according to Roberto Carcangiu, executive chef at the new Academia Barilla culinary center in Parma."

Pardon me? Yes, I know. Country folk don't eat risotto. You know that. I know that. It's the poor magazine that doesn't know that. And no, I've never heard anyone describe a crock pot of pinto beans with ham bone as "quintessential slow food." Oh, and where's Parma? Well, it's not in southern Alabama, sweet friend. It's in Italy. "Country Home" magazine went to Italy to find someone to talk about country food. What a shame. One trip to Palmersville could have given them food fodder for a year. But, no. They had to cross the great pond. Don't even get me started concerning the chilled yellow pepper and garlic soup from the April 2006 issue. Chilled soup? No. I can't even address it. Too painful.

I think we need to write a "group letter" to this sweet though naïve editor. Let's invite her to a West Tennessee bar-b-q potluck in the Smartts' backyard woods. Are you with me? Maybe we'll all end up in an issue of "Country Home." I'll set up the tables and folding chairs, complete with white bed sheet tablecloths. Who's bringing the pinto beans?

Oh No! Spring Means Lawn and Garden Care

I like winter. Everything in our yard is dry and brown…and nobody blames me. It's winter. In winter, everybody knows what to expect. But spring is coming and I'm becoming very afraid. Pretty soon home owners are going to be out mowing and tilling and mulching, like they know what they're doing…and why they're doing it. Many confident homeowners plow through spring as though they actually have a "Lawn and Garden Plan." I'll be honest. We don't have a plan. The winter plan was working really well for us. We did nothing. The lawn did nothing. We were all in perfect agreement.

But winter cannot last. I already see sprigs of green in the front yard. I have a feeling the lawn mower will soon be coming out of winter hibernation. This is bad news for me because I'm afraid of the mower. And riding lawn mowers are like dogs. They can smell fear. We may just let the grass grow.

I'm glad I live in the country. Country folk can live as they please. We can let the grass get too high and say it's "wildlife habitat." No homeowner's association comes around with a clipboard judging our personal taste in lawn care. Whew! That's a relief. Imagine if country folk in my neck of the woods had to undergo the scrutiny some upper crust suburban neighborhoods endure. My goodness. The disassembled 4-wheelers, ceramic roosters, and front yard deer decoys would all be a thing of the past. And you could just plum forget those truck tire flower beds. It would be a crying shame to outlaw a truck tire full of marigolds or a flock of fake geese by the driveway. Rural America would rightfully revolt.

Now that I'm a "country dweller," it's not just lawn care that makes me nervous. I'm afraid of vegetable gardening. Let me re-phrase that. I'm not afraid. I'm lazy and I don't want to do the work required to establish a vegetable garden. There. I said it. Don't dare call my relatives in West Kentucky and relay this information. It's an embarrassment to my heritage. When I was growing up, all my country "kin" put out a garden. There was no discussing it. The ONLY people who didn't put out a garden were people who were not expected to live more than a few months. I'm serious. People would say, "I guess you heard that Uncle Henry is on his death bed." "Yes, Myrtle tells me he didn't even put out sweet corn or yellow squash this year." That settles it. He will be dead soon. If he doesn't die of natural causes, he will die because of gardening failure.

If our lawn fails and the vegetable garden doesn't happen, it's now down to my prowess with spring flowers. Annuals. Perennials. I have no idea what those words mean. I know how to pour water into flower pots. That is my skill. And even with that skill, there must be the accompanying commitment to practice the skill. Many times I have killed living things….not because I did not possess the skill to water, but because for some reason I failed to actually practice the skill of watering. Not this year. This is my year for spring flowers. This is the year I stay committed to my budding and blossoming friends. The radiant colors will be streaming off our porch and flowing effortlessly like a crimson sunset through our flower beds. I believe I'll even acquire an entire fleet of truck tires and fill each one with an abundance of floral finery. A reporter will visit from "Better Homes and Gardens" and stand in speechless awe. People from "town" will start flocking out to our place to observe the sheer wonder of my spring flowers. There's only one down side. The waist-high grass may inhibit the view.

Chapter 10

Paying Tribute

Two Birthmoms...My Heroes

In a few days, millions of moms across the world will be honored. I count it a privilege to be among those moms. My two boys will rise at the crack of dawn and give me a gift and a hug. I'll cry a little and tell them I can't imagine life without them. They might even attempt cooking breakfast for me. Three males in the kitchen. Hmm. This could spell disaster. I wonder if I can convince them that I really am hungry for Raisin Bran.

Mother's Day and Father's Day are extra special occasions in our home. Our journey to parenthood was a long one. For seven years, Mother's Day was a sad reminder that I wasn't a mom. Those of you who have traveled this path know the pain and disappointment I'm writing about. Some of you may still be on the journey. (If you are, please e-mail me. I want to support you!)

I've never been pregnant a day in my life. But, Mother's Day is no longer a day of grieving for me. Eight years ago something miraculous happened. I became a real mom.

A beautiful single college student named Stacy became pregnant in 1995. She was already single parenting a child and she and her parents agreed adoption was the best option. We were with a wonderful adoption agency in the Dallas area. She looked at our profile page and said, "I knew the minute I saw your picture that you were the ones." The first time we met her, I reached out to hug her and there was this bond. Words don't do it justice. Stacy and I loved each other. We would always love each other. We would be linked together for the rest of our lives by this wonderful thing called adoption. She gave Stephen life. We would help him live it.

Two years later, we met Karen. She would be the next special blessing in our lives. She was 35 years old, a college graduate, single parent of a 12 year old. She was a friend of a friend who lived about three hours away. She was pregnant and had decided to place for adoption. She asked her boss if she knew of a Christian couple looking to adopt. It's a long and unbelievable story how we knew Karen's boss. Karen called us and we liked her instantly. We agreed to meet the next week. Again, I reached out to hug her and I felt the same bond. She interviewed us while taking complete notes. She was amazing. It was wonderful. We laughed together and she found our two year old Stephen engaging and entertaining. Karen gave Jonathan life. We would parent him through it.

I'm glad I never got pregnant. I can't imagine not being Stephen and Jonathan's mom. They were more than worth the years of waiting. They are exceptional gifts from the hand of God.

I don't know what you think about adoption. I don't know what you think about women who place babies for adoption. Over the years we've heard a few comments like, "How could anyone just give away their baby?" "I bet she'll regret it someday." "Do you think your kids wonder about their 'real' parents?" Good questions.

If you're curious about adoption or would like more details on our experience, please contact me. Adoption is not an easy choice. Stacy and Karen loved these boys tremendously. Adoption is not a choice made by those who don't love their babies. On both adoption occasions, the birthmoms cried. We cried. Everyone cried. Adoption is emotional and it's not for the faint of heart. They believed they were doing what was right for themselves, for the boys, for us. As for the boys, they understand very clearly about adoption. They grew in Stacy's and Karen's tummies. Stacy and Karen loved them very much but didn't think they would be the best ones to parent them. So, they chose us to be their real mom and dad. My boys and my husband have a special bond. Both boys dream of being a "real man" like Daddy. The boys think Stacy and Karen made a good choice.

For us, it all makes sense. We see God's sovereign hand all over it. These two women got pregnant unprepared for parenting. We were prepared for parenting but couldn't get pregnant. The fact that we all met when we did is a miracle. God has blessed our family tree with two fine sons. But, always at the roots will be Stacy and Karen...our family heroes.

*The names have been changed to protect their privacy.

Tribute to Two "Old" People

I don't know what age you consider "old." Our culture has decided that getting old is a bad thing. So none of us wants to own up to it. I'm not afraid of getting old. I'll never be embarrassed to tell my age. Maybe it's because I've seen the road to retirement paved by two extraordinary individuals. It's time I pay tribute to them. These columns have been filled with stories about my wonderful husband and my two boys. I want to share today about two tremendously gifted individuals. I've been privileged to call them Mom and Dad.

My parents live in a moderate house in a neighborhood that some would say is "going down." My parents don't know what "going down" means. They love their neighborhood. They're both retired teachers. My mom is a brilliant writer and one of the most intelligent people I've ever known. She has a gift for hospitality. When you come to their home for dinner, good smells waft through the air. The table is set and there's a love you can't put your finger on. My dad is a 6 ft. 8 in. juggler, former basketball player, gardener, magician, and a people person. Children are naturally drawn to him. Recently when they saw several neglected children in their neighborhood, my mom developed an after school tutoring program. With approval from parents, my parents hosted children in their home providing good food, help with homework, and needed love and encouragement. A special cake marked each child's birthday.

They currently have a college student living with them. When they told me a young man had moved into the guest room for a year, I didn't blink. I didn't ask if he were paying rent. I knew he wasn't. They wouldn't have considered it. They were helping a needy young man follow his dream. Making room for someone with a need was a common theme during my childhood. People often lived in our guest room or camped out on our couches. Sometimes they were college students. Sometimes they were recovering alcoholics or impoverished people with no place to live. I grew up believing that Christians shared everything they had. Our cars were all available for anyone who needed to drive them. One woman who lived with us managed to put a dent in each of the three cars we owned while she lived with us. We still laugh about it. I was taught that the word "family" extended far beyond the borders of bloodlines.

One day when I was about 12 my dad put $50 in his pocket and said, "Lisa, by the end of the day somebody is probably going to need this." After having spent the entire day with him, no needy people had surfaced. I figured he was mistaken. But he wasn't. As we drove down the interstate at dusk, there was the old car. The hood was up. The young man and woman with several small kids were standing on the shoulder. Dad patted my leg and smiled. With great love, he offered the couple a ride to the repair shop. He never said it out loud, but he paid for all the repairs on the car. He had the money in his account. It made sense to my parents to live this way.

It's not that my parents are unflawed. No. They're flawed. My dad's been known to get a little "hot under the collar" now and then. You don't want to get lost on a family vacation with him. We all know not to sit in his chair or mess with him during the nightly news. Mom's mellow nature keeps her flaws more hidden. Even that is an irritant at times. But I found their flaws easy to forgive. Love has a way of doing that to a person.

Their Christian faith had tremendous impact on me. Jesus of the Bible had not made them cold, condemning, or self-righteous. No. He had the opposite effect. He had made them humble and loving. They had no tolerance for racism, unkind words toward any human being, or gossip. It was impossible to be in their presence and not be drawn to Christ. And people were. They still are.

So consider this my tribute to two special "old" people. Thanks, Mom and Dad. You make getting "old" look good. Who could count the number of lives that have been changed by your grace-filled love? I know of at least one.

Ordinary Heroes

William Butler Smith was going to war. It wasn't by choice. But it wasn't unwillingly either. As a 24-year-old man, he was inducted into the Army of the United States. It was the spring of 1944. He trained at Ft. Bragg, North Carolina, and at Aberdeen Proving Grounds in Maryland. After reaching the rank of Buck Sergeant, he marched from bivouac to Pier 52 in New York City. Red Skelton accompanied the troops as they marched. It was clearly understood that many of the young soldiers would never again return to American soil. But they kept marching. It's not that they were without fear. No. They were human. But they kept marching despite the fear. Duty bound, they boarded a ship headed for the shores of Belgium. Young men were getting ready to be involved in World War II. They could have never been fully prepared for what awaited them.

William Butler Smith was a Tennessee country boy. Unlike some of his comrades, he was leaving a new family behind. A wife and three children were left to wait and wonder. The oldest child was three years old and the baby only six months old when he began his training. But he was confident that his wife, Loreta, would keep the home fires burning. While caring for three small children, she wrote to her soldier husband every day. "Baby Sylvia is walking now." "David is trying to understand why Daddy can't be at home." "Nancy is growing prettier every day." It was all news that William Butler cared deeply about. The letters would be read and re-read. Though he was able to write to his family, they never knew where he was. His younger brother was also serving on the front lines of the war effort, but they never saw each other.

Almost two years after being inducted into the Army, William Butler Smith returned to New York City. The returning soldiers were regarded as heroes. If they went into an eating establishment, an ordinary citizen would often pay for their meal. But, the 24-year-old country boy who had joined the Army was not the 26-year-old man who returned to New York City. No. Now he was a man who had known war. Killing. Fighting. Bloody conflict. He had been a scout and part of his duty had included demolition clean-up after the Battle of the Bulge. He had seen and experienced things he had never imagined. His children were taught not to ask him about his time in the Army. Like many World War II veterans, he came home, worked a job, loved his family…and chose not to speak much about his time at war. If he did speak of it, it was just about funny things that happened or general information.

William Butler Smith's story is not unusual. He fought in World War II. He chose not to talk much about it. But Veteran's Day reminded us to thank the thousands upon thousands of people like him. They marched into service despite the uncertainties which awaited them. And they're still marching today. On Veteran's Day, we reminded our children to be grateful for the service of all our military personnel. We reminded them that many sacrificed their lives. And many are still in harm's way.

William Butler Smith still lives in McMinnville, Tennessee with the love of his life, Loreta. They've been married 66 years. On Veteran's Day our boys called to thank him. They're proud of his service to our country and even prouder that he's their great-grandpa.

"Hug a Teacher" Day

I'm establishing a national holiday. I know. I don't have the authority to establish a national holiday. OK then. I'm establishing a regional holiday. I know. I don't have the authority to establish a regional holiday either. County holiday? City-wide holiday? Nope. OK. I'm starting to feel a little insecure here. Let's see. How about this? As a small-town newspaper columnist, I make a humble suggestion to the readers in Northwest Tennessee. Whew! I decree that this day be declared "Hug a Teacher" Day.

Join me with your personal commitment to the enthusiastic hugging of a teacher. I promise this will be quite easy. When you're going about the course of your regular routine, just hug a teacher. Let me give you an example. While walking through the cereal aisle of the grocery store today, you see Mrs. Smith, your fourth grade teacher. She taught the joys and multiple uses of multiplication. But you were an elementary school rebel. You didn't believe Mrs. Smith in fourth grade. You hated multiplication. Now, you own your own business and use multiplication and percentages every day. Reach out and give Mrs. Smith a big hug, would you? Thank you.

Let's examine another scenario. You live down the street from Mrs. Jones. Mrs. Jones has taught high school English for many years. In a great epiphany, you realize that one of the reasons the children on your street are literate and well-spoken has to do with Mrs. Jones' commitment to drill proper use of the language into their little MTV-filled minds. Wow! You realize what a challenge Mrs. Jones faces every day. The culture has filled teenagers' minds with SO many distractions. Yet, every day Mrs. Jones continues the vigilant pursuit of great language usage! Let's give Mrs. Jones a little appreciation, shall we?   Throw on your bunny slippers and run down the street and give Mrs. Jones a big ol' hug on behalf of civilized society! (Please do this before dark so Mrs. Jones won't feel compelled to call law enforcement and have you arrested. Being arrested on "Hug a Teacher" Day would be a crying shame. And think how your elementary school guidance teacher, Mrs. Morgan, would feel when she read it in the paper.)

If you currently have children in the school system, write a note expressing your appreciation to their teachers and administrators. If the thought of writing a note makes you turn pale and lifeless, express your appreciation in some other creative way. If you're not feeling very enthusiastic about this project, ask yourself the following questions: "What if I spent all day everyday with twenty-two 5-year-olds? What if during the course of that day someone expected me to teach those 5-year-olds the basics of phonics and language usage AND the concept of numbers and spatial understanding? What if while I was teaching the basics of phonics and language usage and math concepts, I was also expected to keep Johnny from pulling Susan's hair barrette out of her hair because every time he pulls her barrette out, he's not showing respect for others and it always makes Susan cry in that high-pitched little girl wail which breaks a vase on my desk?" What's that? You say you're feeling excited and even ENTHUSIASTIC about "Hug a Teacher" Day? Great! I knew you would!

OK. The rules are simple. Find a teacher. Hug a teacher. If you're not a "hugging" person, no need to feel bad or seek therapy. A hearty handshake with a kind word will suffice. Before I close, I'd like to include a special thank-you to my wildly creative sixth grade English teacher, Mrs. Thomason. I'd also like to thank my mom who is a retired teacher and the best writer I've ever known. Both of you showed me the power of words.

A Tribute to Soldiers and Military Families

We were pondering plans for Memorial Day weekend. A family camping trip? A Sunday School Class picnic? A weekend getaway for two? The possibilities were endless and all sounded enjoyable. Then something happened. My eyes were opened.

While speaking at an event at the Union City Library, a dear lady gave me a precious gift. Her daughter had written a book about military families and the challenges they face. My Memorial Day plans were about to change.

The book, "Homefires: War through the eyes of a military wife" written by Sherry Hines, brought laughter and tears. I wasn't prepared for the rich experience brought about by such a simple book. The passion. The sacrifice. The stark reality.

Her recounting of military life provided a valuable wake-up call. Like so many Americans, I sometimes forget we're at war. No grocery items are rationed. No shortage of food or services. Life moves on for so many of us...while thousands serve in desolate and difficult conditions in a dry and desert land, miles and miles from home.

I wake up every morning and serve breakfast to my family. My children go to school and I rarely worry about their safety. My husband drives into our driveway every day between 5:30 and 5:40. We eat supper soon after his arrival. Relishing the warmth of home ...while thousands wait for dads and moms to come home from a dangerous and uncertain life of service.

I complain about gas prices and slow internet service...while a family somewhere in America learns that their loved one is dead.

My kids complain when Daddy has to go on a business trip. He'll be gone two nights. "It's not fair!" they protest...while many children wait months for a needed hug or game of pitch.

And some parents and sons and daughters never come home. They make the ultimate sacrifice.

I would like to offer the following excerpt from page 11 of Mrs. Hines' book:

The Knock

The mother hears the knock at the door, wondering who could it be this late. Soldiers? Why would soldiers be at my door? My son? No, not my son, there must be a mistake. I just heard from him. In her mind she sees flashes of memories: a toddler taking his first steps, a small boy starting kindergarten, his dirty ball uniform, his first girlfriend, teaching him to drive, in his cap and gown at graduation. Watching the boy leave for basic, knowing he will come back a man. But the one that stays, is the last one she has.

The wife hears the knock at the door. She knew about the accident, but didn't want to believe it could be him. Even now as she hears it, it couldn't be him. If she doesn't answer it, will that make it not true? In her mind she sees flashes of memories: the day they met, their first kiss, seeing him so young and happy, on one knee asking for her hand, their wedding day with him waiting at the end of the aisle. The day her son was born, looking as though he is the only man to father a child, pride shining in his eyes. But the one that stays, is the last one she has.

Thank you, Sherry Hines. Thank you for the much-needed reminder. America is at war. Soldiers need our support.

Families need our support. We must never forget those who've sacrificed their lives in military service. Memorial Day? This year we'll be sure to remember.

Hurricane Heroes

Lots of people never make the news. Take my dad, for instance. He's 71 and I don't think I've ever seen him interviewed on a newscast. He probably never will be. There are plenty of people who have more "position" and "prestige" who will continue to talk on TV about the recent hurricane tragedy. They'll be wearing a tie when they use phrases like "should have" and "could have" and "disappointed in the response." That's fine. Let them talk. There are others you'll never see on TV because they're too busy DOING what "should have" and "could have" been done. Many of our friends are on their way to Mississippi and Louisiana driving trucks filled with supplies. Many of our Texas friends are opening their homes and perfect strangers are now becoming members of their family. They're probably not going to be on CNN tonight. I doubt they really care about making the national news.

Over the course of my life, I've witnessed my dad help to re-build structures in Florida after Hurricane Andrew. He and my mom have stood in water shoveling out an old woman's basement in Iowa after a devastating flood. They've worked to provide relief in the poorest areas of the United States. They've spent countless weeks on Indian reservations and my dad has been involved in building projects around the world. They've taken in refugees in every form and fashion. They don't make it a topic of conversation because it doesn't seem a big deal to them. It doesn't make newscasts because it's not very exciting press.

We're seeing a lot of footage right now about the devastation in Louisiana and Mississippi. Maybe governmental mistakes were made. No doubt they were. I feel for the personal suffering of some of our poorest American citizens. If you can watch the TV and not get tears in your eyes, something is wrong. People are suffering. Tragedy always brings suffering. Much press has been given to the mistakes made. Let's give some press to the thousands upon thousands of people who are reaching out to help.

It was painful to hear a European newscaster say that America has a lot to answer for in regard to this tragedy. I'm glad that many of my friends and relatives were too busy helping the victims…to have had time to hear the criticism. A woman, who was a hotel guest in New Orleans, said that she looked out her hotel window and was SO disappointed in the relief efforts. She described that scene as being totally "unorganized." Let's be sure to call her to help "organize" the next hurricane. Tragedy is not easily organized. Tragedy is messy and unpredictable. Tragedy brings suffering and disappointment. We're so used to being able to control everything. We sometimes forget there are things we can't control.

I'm not going to focus on criticism in the midst of this chapter of American suffering. It seems a waste of time…especially in light of the incredible efforts Americans are making. Instead, I'm going to rejoice in the thousands upon thousands of people who care deeply and give sacrificially. If you've spent most of your time criticizing what others should have done and questioning what our country should have done, ask a new question instead. What can I do?

Chapter 11

Sometimes Life Hurts: A Serious Look at Suffering

A Sad Farewell

If you're looking for a smile or a chuckle in today's column, forgive me. I'm sad today. I can't find it in my heart to write anything funny. I just returned from a funeral. My sweet friend and neighbor buried her son today. It's a painful story...but it's one worth telling.

There once was a little boy who ran through the woods. He ran through the very same woods my boys are running through today. The little boy's grandfather told me he would sometimes return from the depths of the forest with a stick and say, "PaPaw, I killed a bear." I smile because I hear the same adventurous stories from my own little boys. The woods draw out the "adventure" in a child's heart. It's a beautiful thing.

This little boy liked to play sports and tease his sister. He was a regular kid. He played high school football and enjoyed friends. He had two loving parents who modeled kindness, integrity, and work ethic. They were imperfect parents...just like us. He had a loving and connected extended family. He was blessed.

One day he got involved with illegal drugs...and the story took a terrible turn. The boy who once ran through the woods seemed to be turning into a different boy. Loving family members and concerned friends seemed powerless to help. It was as though this boy had fallen into a great abyss...and those he loved watched in desperation as he spiraled downward. They reached out their hands from the edge of the abyss even yelling out to say, "Grab hold! Hold on! We'll help you get out!" But the abyss of drug addiction and rebellion seemed to be pulling ever downward.

Despite the downward spiral, he married a lovely young woman and spent four years in the military. They had three beautiful and talented daughters. Everyone figured that becoming a father would weaken the pull of the addictions. It did sometimes. There were good times and times of great hope. Those are the times to be remembered.

The little boy who once played in the woods my boys play in died Monday morning in an altercation with local police. It was a tragedy of epic proportions and on so many levels. As a mother, I look into the eyes of my little boys and I dream big dreams for them...dreams my friend had for her son, too. I feel only a tiny portion of what my friend must be feeling today...the sadness, the loss, the awareness of dreams that never became reality.

As I write this, I watch my own little boys out the window. The forest ablaze with fall color is the backdrop for their adventures. They're clad in rubber boots and accompanied by their ever-faithful dog companions. They run with an almost limitless energy and smile as though all is right with the world. Sometimes they wear super hero costumes and engage in the battle between good and evil. Tears well up in my eyes because I know the battle is real.

In old westerns, the plot was easy to follow. The bad guys wore black hats. The good guys wore white. Reality is much more complicated than that. We all have a few black hats in our closet. That propensity should provide us with needed caution and appropriate humility.

God, in His infinite wisdom, does not show us the future. He does not guarantee our personal pleasure nor does He insure that our children's dreams will all be fulfilled. He does not promise that we will not experience grief or even embarrassment over the choices our children make. He does promise mercy and forgiveness for those who place their faith in Christ. That's the greatest gift I can think of. The boy in this story had placed his trust in Christ's mercy and forgiveness. He recognized his need for it. The mercy of Christ will carry him in the same way that mercy carries me. The mercy will forgive his atrocities...in the same way it forgives my atrocities. And the tears of sorrow will be turned to tears of joy.

Human Tragedy

I can't think of one funny or engaging thing to write. Not one. Humor and creativity are the farthest things from my mind. A little girl in our community died a tragic death. A family is grieving. Tears hit the computer keys as I'm reminded of that almost-horrible risky love that comes with parenting. I cry again as I travel back a few years when I got the phone call that my friend's 7-year old daughter had been killed in a tragic accident. Numb. Angry. Devastated. I remember the stupid and ridiculous things some people naively said during that tragedy. "It will all work out for the best." "God must have needed her more than we did." "Time heals all wounds." "Her death will certainly make people re-evaluate their priorities and look more closely at their own lives." Rubbish all. Rubbish.

In contrast to such trite comments, I think of the Bible's loving admonition to rejoice with those who rejoice and weep with those who weep. When it comes to rejoicing, I see the picture of a party where everyone is congratulating the guest of honor. High-fiving! Three cheers! Here's a toast! The rejoicing produces smiles and back slaps. It's clearly a time for celebrating.

When I think of weeping with those who weep, I think of a funeral. Crying. Wailing. Saying with our actions, "We are so very sad. There is intense pain here because you lost someone you held dear, most dear." The call is clearly to share in their sufferings, not solve their sufferings. We get into trouble when we try to explain human suffering. It is beyond us. Some well-meaning people have had difficulty grasping this concept. They feel compelled to give a reason. They believe an explanation would "make it all better." But an explanation wouldn't make it better. God knew it wouldn't. He calls us to weep with those who weep. That's why I think it's healthy to say, "What tragedy! What loss! What pain! What anger you must be feeling!" Are we so afraid of things we don't understand that we have to offer self-imposed explanations upon a sovereign God whose ways are so much higher than our own?

This community is the most loving and supportive place I've ever lived. I've no doubt the grieving family has felt a greater outpouring of love and support than they could have ever imagined. But if you're tempted to provide an explanation or a "reason" for what happened, please don't. Weeping is the need for the day.

Madison Fagan is rejoicing in heaven. What a glorious and awe-inspiring thought. We can't even fathom the pure joy of her experience. But her family members are terribly sad. They miss her. Some of you know first-hand the horrid gut-wrenching pain of grief because you have walked the path. Lots of crying. Lots of "what if" questions. Wondering how the rest of the world goes shopping, does homework, and acts as though our loved one is not gone. Shortly after my friend in Texas lost her daughter, she described the grief in this way, "I wake up every day and for just a moment, I believe it was all a terrible dream. But my feet hit the floor and I realize her death is reality. So I sit on the side of the bed and have a good morning cry." That is the nature of grief. We don't solve it. We experience it.

Hope for Middle School Girls

It's an educational experience to sit outside a middle school at 3:00...a psychological study of epic proportions. Some things never change. I was sitting in front of our local middle school recently and observed clusters of kids in every size and description. Some looked confident. Others looked scared. One young girl stands out in my mind...because she looked like me. I wanted to run up to this young lady and hug her and never let go. I wanted to tell her to hang in there and not give up. I wanted to remind her that this is just middle school. That's all it is.

As I observed this young lady, it was 1976 all over again and I was in 8th grade. We had just moved from a small Kentucky town to a large school in Texas. I was a tall, strangely disproportioned, insecure 13-year-old. That's the nice way of saying it. Just thinking about being 13 makes me want to see a therapist and eat a doughnut. For all you teenage girls out there, I'm sending you a hug...and a message.

The only thing that saved my life in eighth grade was joining the Jr. High Speech Club. Mrs. Harpool single-handedly saved my disproportioned and dysfunctional life that year. I wish she were alive today. I would send her flowers. Mrs. Harpool didn't seem to see a tall, insecure, strange-looking eighth grader. She saw someone else.

She pulled me aside one day before a speech competition and said, "Lisa, stand tall. You have a gift. You have presence. You can do this." Just writing that makes me want to cry. My parents believed those same things about me. The other eighth graders saw someone completely different. I stuck out like a sore thumb.

191

When I look back on eighth grade, there's a strange realization that hits me. I was succeeding in speech and drama competitions and doing well in academics. But it wasn't enough. I would have GLADLY traded all of it...just to be beautiful for one day. I didn't want to be a success in speech or academics. I wanted to be beautiful and popular. I wanted to be liked by boys and respected by the other girls. I wanted to be a trendsetter and a "somebody." Everyone said that junior high trauma was "character building." I didn't want character. I wanted to steer clear of "character building" in any way I could.

I never succeeded in the "junior high world." It wasn't my destiny. I never went to a dance. No boys ever called. The girls managed to set their own trends, without my input. I know there are girls out there who are having the same experience in middle school right now. Lean in close...and listen carefully. Take my hand. Someday it won't matter. I promise.

This column wouldn't be complete without a word to those who are on the middle school "inside track." If you've managed to steer clear of the "ugly stage" and people consider you a "trend setter," you have an opportunity to do something really valuable today. You see, there's a girl, probably in one of your classes or in your neighborhood. You need to pay attention. This girl has something valuable to contribute to your life. She can teach you things and bring a ray of diversity to your life. If you ignore her, middle school won't be a time of "character building" for you...and you'll have to go through "character building" later on in life...when I PROMISE it will be more painful. If you alienate people or treat them poorly, you'll go through an "ugly stage" that is far more destructive and harder to shed.

As for the tall and insecure girl who was an 8th grader in 1976, everything turned out remarkably well. She dated very little...and married a prince. She was never in the spotlight...and learned to love people who leaned against the wall. The world never considered her beautiful...and she learned the precious art of conversation. She was never a trendsetter...and she learned to look at eternity. If she had to go back to eighth grade, it might be tempting to try to change the way history unfolded. But looking back, she wouldn't change a thing.

When Mother's Day Brings Pain

You've seen the commercial. A beautiful model opens her Mother's Day gifts while surrounded by her three cherub children and her adoring and sensitive husband who looks like he walked off the cover of GQ magazine. Happy Mother's Day, America. For some people, this may be Sunday's scenario. For a lot of you, it won't even come close.

Some of you are hurting. Mother's Day brings with it a special sadness for a large segment of the population. The world promises it's a day of celebration. For a lot of you, it will be a day of mourning. It's time we acknowledge that pain.

I think of my friend in Texas who hates shopping for Mother's Day cards. She said,"All the cards say things like, 'You were always there for me, Mom. You were my inspiration.' My mom wasn't there for me. She never inspired me. She treated me poorly. Eventually she walked out on me. Where is the card that says, 'I wish things had been different'? I guess they don't make that card. I always just buy a card that says, 'I love you, Mom.' And I cry when I mail it." Her words still pierce my heart.

I think of the moms who've lost children. My sweet neighbor lost her son this year. A dear friend in Texas experienced the tragic death of her six-year-old a few years ago. Many of you have walked this path of pain. Mother's Day becomes an annual reminder of the child you would so love to hug...just one more time. When standing with my friend at her little girl's casket, she tearfully said, "Look, Lisa, there's still some finger paint under her fingernails. We painted together on Saturday. I would give anything to finger paint with her...just one more time." There are no words to share with those of you who have walked this path. To you I offer a prayer for God's comfort and a terribly inadequate, "I'm sorry."

I think of the birthmoms in the world who have placed babies for adoption. These are the courageous women who experienced the pain of personal loss believing it would be gain for others. I especially think of the two precious and wonderful birthmoms who gave birth to our boys. I think about what one of these women said years ago, "When I remember him, sometimes I get sad. Then I look at his picture and the life that he has and I say, 'God is good.'" To all birthmoms out there, I'm sending you a hug on behalf of every couple like us who are miraculously celebrating Mother's Day this year. The words "thank you" are painfully inadequate.

Some of you have experienced the death of your mother. Perhaps your mom was the one person who understood you and your dreams. When life was hard, she was the one who always whispered in your ear, "You can do it. Hang in there." On Mother's Day, you remember what it's like to live without the one person who knew what you were thinking. Even surrounded by friends and family, there is a special loneliness. She left a void that you know will never be filled by another. So you relish in her influence and you smile at the fond memories. But you wish you could sit on the front porch with her...just one more time.

Some of you feel the crushing blow of regret this Mother's Day. Your kids are grown but there'll be no special honors on Sunday. No cards. No phone calls. No words of praise. You wonder if you failed as a mom. Maybe you were selfish, or chemically dependent, or mentally unstable when your children were little. And now you sometimes daydream that you can go back and start all over again. You wake up and realize it cannot happen. Life is as it is. Rather than going back, you're left with asking adult children for forgiveness. You're not sure how to do it. For you, I pray for courage. There is hope.

Some of you were great moms who did everything you could to love and cherish the sweet little ones God gave you…but those little ones grew up and rebelled. You had big dreams for your children. They settled for far less. And the world doesn't seem to know your pain…or your shame. You wonder if anyone understands.

Many women across the world will be shedding the tears I shed for seven Mother's Days in a row, until that wonderful year I finally became a mom. These are the tears of unplanned childlessness. Many of you have dreamed of being a mom since your childhood days of playing with dolls. Having babies seemed so easy for the vast majority of people. You had no idea it could be so complicated. You dream of swing sets and messy baby food and funny Christmas pictures. But when you wake up, you feel the pain of reality. No one calls you "Mommy." I know. I remember.

Corsages will soon immerge and special dinners will be prepared. But many of you will take a few moments to find a box of tissue and a quiet place. You'll shed tears of sorrow at what is or was or could have been. Happy Mother's Day…You are not alone.

Teaching Kids about Tragedy

We allowed our boys to watch the evening news the day that thirty-three people died in Virginia. The four of us sat in silence as the details unfolded on the screen. Later, at the supper table, Phil and I expressed our deep sorrow for the families of the victims. We asked the boys a simple question, "How do you think the families feel right now—the families who are finding out that their college student has died?"

Their answer, "Real sad. Really sad."

Tragedy happens in this world. People die. People do bad things. Our boys, 9 and 11, are starting to figure out that this world is not a perfect place. Not even close. At one point, I said, "I feel sorry for one set of parents most of all."

"Who?"

"The parents of the shooter."

My older son looked puzzled. "How can you feel sorry for them? Their son is the one who did it, Mom!"

That's when we explained about parental love. As parents, our greatest desire is for our children to grow up to be productive, loving, stable adults. If one of our boys were killed in a rampage like the one at Virginia Tech, we would be forever grief-stricken. But if he were the one who had caused the death of others, the grief would be FAR worse. Thirty-two innocent people died while going about their daily activities. One person died after claiming the lives of others. To find out that the shooter was your son would have to be a parent's greatest nightmare, bar none.

No one understands what was going through the mind of the young college student as he gunned down his peers. Television personalities pontificate night and day about the possibilities of mental illness, substance abuse, a love gone wrong. But no one really knows. And that's what we told our boys. Sometimes really bad things happen and they are not easy to understand, even for adults. Some experiences defy explanation.

One thing we do know for sure is that fear is not the answer to tragedy. We don't want our boys to be afraid to try new things or to go to new places. Life was meant to be experienced and relished. Physical safety is not a guarantee for any human being on earth and we want our boys to clearly understand that. Besides, if physical safety is the supreme goal of life, we should all board up our houses and lock the doors. And even then, we could die of a heart attack or a plane could crash through the roof at any moment. I'm getting on an airplane in the morning to fly to Texas to speak at a women's retreat. The plane could go down shortly after take-off. I could be side-swiped on the way to Nashville. Phil and the boys could experience a tragic accident while I'm gone. We've never said to our children, "Don't worry. God will protect Mommy while she's on the airplane. He'll bring her back safely." No. God has never promised physical safety to me or to my family. We have a promise far greater and more valuable through Christ. And it's that promise that keeps us from walking in fear or dread. This life is just a vapor. The next one lasts forever.

Chapter 12

Miscellaneous Tidbits on Life's Journey

Some Things Don't Make Sense

Some things don't make sense. White couches. Dog sweaters. Carpet in the dining room. Low-calorie chocolate. These are just some of the many mysteries of our American way of life.

Let's start with white couches, shall we? I looked up the word "couch" in the Webster's Dictionary and found the following definition: an article of furniture on which one may sit or lie down. OK. That proves my point. Couches are for putting your feet on. Couches are for Sunday afternoon naps. However, there's a conspiracy taking shape in this great land of ours. Some people don't want you to embrace and experience the true purpose of a couch. Hence, the invention of the WHITE couch. Here's the truth of the matter. The white couch was invented by people who don't want snoring family members in the living room. People buy white couches so they can walk in the living room and say, "What are you thinking? Get your feet off that stellar white couch and go sleep on the back porch." When this type of verbal shaming is ineffective, white couch owners resort to covering the couch with an extra-crunchy heavy-duty clear plastic cover. And all decent nap-taking Americans know that's a low blow.

Dog sweaters. Explain this to me. Feel free to send an e-mail or call me at home and enlighten me. Dogs are born with fur. Dogs don't care about clothes or high fashion. They don't want shoes, purses, or college funds. A friend once told me that her dog actually loved dressing up in his sweaters and little doggy jackets. I smiled and nodded my head. I couldn't bear to break it to her. I knew that her little Fido, like all dogs, was simply day-dreaming about a pound of raw bacon wrapped around a dead squirrel. Don't worry, Fido. Your secret is safe with me.

Carpet in the dining room. This concept was invented by someone who likes to stir up controversy between parents and kids. The person who thought of carpet in the dining room is living in exile somewhere--laughing about how gullible Americans are. If you have clean carpet in your dining room, it means one of two things. Either you don't eat at home or you daily threaten your family members with a super strength Dust Buster. Neither option is ideal. Dining room carpet should have a few stains on it. I feel sorry for kids whose parents insist on owning a white couch AND maintaining clean dining room carpet. Let's be honest. These are the same parents who are constantly squirting hand sanitizer on their kids. I don't even have time to address the hand sanitizer issue. It's a humor novel just waiting to be written. "Here, Junior. You hugged Aunt Bessie. Let me sanitize you with an antibacterial squirt. Wait! Colleen, you opened a library book. Let's get those germs under control, shall we?" Out-of-control antibacterial squirting. Such a shame. Parents, I love you enough to tell the truth. You're going to end up on national TV someday. Your kids are going to write a book called, "Living Too Clean...How Touch Therapy Helped Me Overcome my Fear of Humans." Go ahead and take your best suit to the cleaners. You're gonna meet Oprah.

Low-calorie chocolate. This needs no detailed explanation. Low-calorie chocolate is morally wrong. Chocolate is chocolate. Fat, sugar, caffeine. These are the things that separate chocolate from kiwi fruit and rice cakes. Low-fat, sugar-free wafer-like items are NOT chocolate simply because they have been carefully dipped into a substance that is brown. No. No. A thousand times no.

Telling little kids not to get dirty. Silent e at the end of words. Low-carb pancakes. These are the things that awaken newspaper columnists in the middle of the night. Bottled water? Don't even get me started.

Tanning Beds and Time Travel

Tanning beds. I don't get it. I know that somewhere in America there is someone who can explain this phenomenon to me in terms I can understand. But I haven't met that person yet. Yesterday I was waiting for both my boys to get their hair cut and was making mental notes of the cultural experience surrounding me. Scores of people were coming in to wait their turn for the tanning beds. Young people. Old people. Men. Women. Pretty people. Plain people. People in great need of the tanning bed experience.

I told the owner at the check-out counter that I was AMAZED at the number of people in Weakley County who had obviously been born the wrong color. He smiled and said it was a booming business. This got me thinking. I've always been fascinated with the concept of time travel. I don't believe you can actually create a time machine that can transport you to another era, but I love movies that involve time travel. I think they can teach us a lot.

I've often wished I could go back to the 1800's for just a day. I wouldn't loiter because the sheer work load of the average woman then would probably hospitalize me. But I'm fascinated to know what a day would be like in a completely different time.

I think it would be equally fascinating for someone from the late 1800's to come spend a day with me, don't you? I know the first place I would take that weary time traveler. I know just the place where my friend from the 1800's could get an up-close look at the culture. We'd make a trip to the local beauty shop for an explanation of the tanning beds. It would go something like this:

203

These are small closet rooms we use for cooking people until they turn another color. Most people here in Weakley County were born a slightly wrong color. Here's how it works: They take their clothes off and put them on that chair. Sometimes they pay money for grease to rub into their skin. The grease causes their bodies to cook more evenly. Then they crawl into this big metal machine. They pull the top down until it's really close to their skin and light bulbs come on. There's no way of knowing for sure when they've cooked enough, but 15 minutes seems to be the trend. At the end of the 15 minutes, they pull the big lid off and put their clothes back on. I've never seen someone look a different color when they come out. But they tell me it's a progressive experience that happens over time.

Oh no. This is not punishment for any crime committed. No. You don't understand what I'm saying. These folks voluntarily pay money to be cooked in this fashion.

Why? They're the wrong color. Haven't you been listening to anything I've explained? These people were born the wrong color. They need to be a different color. Why a different color? Well. Isn't that obvious? Uh. I mean, haven't you ever looked at magazines or TV shows? You haven't. Okay. Well then, just stop and think about it for a moment. I mean, don't you wish you could be a different color? Wouldn't you be willing to pay to be a different color? You wouldn't? Clearly you lack a proper understanding of the culture. You see, someone somewhere decides the right color. We don't have a choice in that. Once the color is decided, it's pretty much decided. Look around. We're all falling in line. Okay. Well. I can see you're not going to be convinced. That's fine. Let's bug out of here and go grab some lunch. How do you feel about low-carb wraps?

Anti-Aging Solution? No Thanks

Newsflash! I don't have to get old. You don't have to get old. It's no longer a requirement. I received a card in the mail that says I can turn back the hands of time. It said it right there in brilliant color, "Lisa, you can turn back the hands of time." Can you believe it? They even knew my name. They must have known that lately my lipstick has been traveling up my nose through a new super highway. But, no more. I can buy their anti-aging cream and be thirty again or even twenty. The reason their product works so well is that it contains "Triple Age Defense Technology." Yes, triple. It doesn't just double the defense against aging. This amazing product metaphorically puts three 300-lb. defensive linemen on the project and there is no way aging is gonna slide in on those guys. Triple defense. Now, if that's not worth $49.99 of our hard-earned dollars, I don't know what is. Oh, and that's not all. I read in a magazine recently that I can dress a certain way to take 10 or even 15 years off my age in this new year.

A journalistic experiment is definitely in order. I need to get up on an average Tuesday morning, smear the anti-aging cream all over my face and body, squeeze my everything into some new jeans and stroll into downtown Dresden. If you see a shiny-looking, tall, fat woman strolling the streets of Dresden dressed in low rider jeans and a denim jacket, just smile and wave, folks. Just smile and wave. People would probably drive by and say, "Look at that 43-year-old woman trying to look 30."And what would that accomplish? If you can think of something, let me know.

Anti-aging. I don't even understand the term. For Pete's sake, what's wrong with aging? Are young people smarter? Are young people wiser? Are young people experienced? No. So, why in the world would I want to be younger? Why would I want to digress rather than progress? Why would I want to oppose the very forces that will bring the wisdom and experience I need? Why would I want to give up my chance to mentor a younger generation? Mind boggling.

My mom is in her seventies now. Gray hair. Wrinkles. Daddy says she's beautiful and he's right. A brilliant writer, she radiates kindness and hospitality. She doesn't use anti-aging products because she doesn't need triple defense against something so normal and natural. This life will eventually be over. But a richer one is yet to come.

I was blessed recently to have lunch with some dear older ladies who inspired me. Our hostess was a lovely Dresden woman in her 80's. She was beautiful. Her hospitality radiated her home as she served us a lovely meal and delighted us with stories. I was by far the junior member of the group. Most of the other ladies had begun raising their families long before I was born. I was in awe. In awe of their experiences. In awe of their laughter and perspective. In awe of their lives. In awe of their continued focus on others and not themselves. Anti-aging? No thanks. Turn back the hands of time? I'll pass. It's onward and upward for me. I need the wisdom age brings.

A Cure for the Whining Disease

"Stop whining." It's probably one of the most spoken phrases in our country, especially by parents. When we have to deny our boys candy before dinner, it's as though they've been sent to Outer Mongolia with no winter coats. If we say, "No more TV today," it's like we've cut off their food supply. No more. Even as I'm writing this, the boys are outside helping my husband haul firewood. Our goal is simple: Work the whining right out of them. Tire their little male bodies until they only have enough energy left to speak respectfully to their wonderful parents. I'll let you know how it goes.

I'm on a mission and I'm rallying your support. I want to establish a movement in this great country of ours, "Stop Whining in 2005." I envision this simple phrase on billboards, t-shirts, bumper stickers, and pot holders. Maybe we could even convince a famous country singer to write a song about the many pitfalls of whining. Here are a few lyric ideas, "Please stop whining while I'm dining." "When you whine, I'm sad you're mine." "If you insist on your complaining, I'll sleep outside even though it's raining." I know. Don't quit my day job.

I wish I were just talking about kids. Adults can also fall prey to a rather contagious case of the "whining disease." I was once checking out at a large retail facility. The checker and I began to discuss grocery shopping and what a hassle it can be. I was joining right in with how hard it is to drag my kids out and pile the cart up with food. She said, "Well, the WORST part is after you get home. You've got to unload all this food and put it away. That's the part I dread the most." That's when it hit me. We are SO prosperous that we've lost our minds! Here's what the checker and I were really complaining about, "We have so much money to spend on food that we pile our cart up each week. We take this bounty of food and load it into a car that will drive us right up next to our house. We then have the privilege of walking all of six grueling steps into our home to put the food away. This happens every week because we have never missed a meal." Yeah. That's a tragedy alright.

Many of you have had to face some real difficulties in this life. Terminal illness. Teen rebellion. Substance abuse. Depression. Loss of a special friend or loved one. Those issues are not what I'm talking about today. I'm talking about those little irritants we need to learn to let go of.

Let's be honest. Whining is just a bad habit. Will someone please invent a patch that would give us a light electric shock every time we complain about the weather, a slow driver, or cellulite? Until the patch comes along, I think we're all going to have to go "cold turkey."

Okay, friends. Raise your right hand and repeat after me, "No more whining and complaining." I'm serious. I'm in if you are. Let's join the West Tennessee "Stop Whining in 2005" Massive Societal Movement. Telemarketers? Not worth complaining about. Socks on the floor? Not even close. A faithful spouse who doesn't take out the trash? Please. A fender bender where everyone walks away? A blessing. A meal that doesn't turn our perfectly? A good laugh. Waiting in line at the grocery store? An opportunity to be friendly. A friend who makes an insensitive comment? Forgive and let go. The waitress brought the wrong order? Hardly a national tragedy. Your husband or wife left out the peanut butter? Smile and put it away.

Join me in spreading an "attitude of gratitude" throughout West Tennessee. Help start an epidemic.

What's "Trailer Trash"?

I'm confused. It's the term "trailer trash." I don't get it. Maybe some of you readers can enlighten my mind in regard to this subject. I've heard this term thrown around quite a bit lately and I'm simply at a loss as to what it means. It seems the term usually comes up in reference to human beings. But I must be mistaken.

My family and I were blessed to live in a trailer park in Texas for six years. It was a great experience. I'm serious. We had a wonderful 16X80 home on wheels. Our friends affectionately called it the "Mobile Mansion." We were content there. We were more than content. We were deliriously happy. When we prepared to move to Tennessee, our kids begged us not to sell it. They desperately wanted us to pull it to Tennessee. How much cooler could it be than to live in a house on wheels?

We met some wonderful and interesting people during our time in the trailer park. There was a single mom named Nancy and her kids. Money was tight. They had a hard time. But, trash? No. They in no way resembled a wadded up paper bag or discarded milk carton.

There was our next door neighbor who was a young guy on disability from the military. He had depression problems and needed a lot of love. He was a good neighbor. He had some problems. But, trash? No. There was nothing about him that resembled an empty soda can or a used paper plate.

Rachel and Jeremy lived in the trailer park, too. They had three small kids. They had college degrees and he had a good job. They paid cash for a mobile home rather than buy into a life of indebtedness so common among people their age. We respected them greatly. There was nothing about them that resembled potato peelings or coffee grounds.

There were even some people in our park addicted to illegal substances. Some were alcoholics. Others were on welfare. But, trash? Not even close. They all looked like people to us and to our kids. We were one of them. We are one of them.

I still don't get it. What could people possibly mean by the term "trailer trash"? It reminds me of 1st grade when little "Sally Somebody Special" would go around the playground shouting "Mary's got cooties. Mary's got cooties." Mary was usually one of the poorer kids. Sally thought if she made fun of Mary, it would make Sally look cool. It did…in 1st grade. She was immature and naïve. And so were we.   Sally believed the only way to make herself look valuable was to de-value someone else. We bought into it.   In adulthood we figured out her gig, didn't we? Sally wasn't cooler. She was insecure.   The only way she could bolster her standing in society was to find someone weaker on the "social chain" and draw attention to that person.

We all make mistakes. I make a lot of them. Sometimes we're just blind to the things we say and do that are inappropriate to the values we hold. If you believe God created every person with a purpose, you can't possibly use the term "trash" to describe a human being. If you understand your own potential for weakness and inadequacy, certainly you'll have compassion on others' weaknesses and inadequacies. If you've called people "trash" before, don't feel bad. Just stop doing it. And as far as "trailer trash" goes, our family has had some experience with it. We carried it to the curb every Thursday.